D0207567

The Anatomy of Skiing

R. J. Sanders, M.D.

Illustrated by R. G. Delmendo

Vintage Books
A Division of Random House/New York

FIRST VINTAGE BOOKS EDITION, October 1979

Copyright © 1976, 1979 by Richard J. Sanders, M.D.

All rights reserved under International and Pan-American Copyright Conventions. Published in the United States by Random House, Inc., New York, and in Canada by Random House of Canada Limited, Toronto. Originally published in another version by Golden Bell Press in 1976.

Grateful acknowledgment is made to the following for permission to reprint previously published material:

Figures from *The Complete Guide to Cross-Country Skiing and Touring* by Martin Luray and Art Tokle, with permission of the authors.

Design by Stephanie Tevonian

Library of Congress Cataloging in Publication Data

Sanders, Richard J

The anatomy of skiing.

Reprint of the 1976 ed. published by Golden Bell Press.
Includes index.
1. Skis and skiing—Physiological aspects. 2. Anatomy, Human.
I. Title.
RC1220.S5S26 1979 796.9'3 79-11421
ISBN 0-394-72975-7

Manufactured in the United States of America

To Bernard Z. Lande (1927–1978)

I would like to thank Cathy Erceg, Sara Gustafson, Dr. Arnold Heller, Burt Langfur, Hal Langfur, Dr. Harold Leight, Dr. Bruce Paton, Barbara Phillips, Edie Resnick, Barry Segal, and Tom Stein for their critiques, suggestions and ideas. The Lande Manufacturing Company kindly loaned the use of their facilities for photographing. And an extra word of appreciation to my secretary, Nelda Brown

R.J.S.

Contents

Part III: Cross-Country Skiing

Part IV: Health and Safety on the Slopes

Introduction

The idea of writing a book on skiing occurred to me several years ago, when I was teaching my children to ski. I thought others might benefit from my experience of explaining snowplow, stem, and parallel turns to them. I began work on a manuscript, but didn't get too far until a friend gave me a book on tennis called *Racket Work: The Key to Tennis* by John Barnaby. This book totally changed my tennis game, which until then had been poor, inconsistent, and showed no improvement in spite of professional lessons. Barnaby explained that the whole game of tennis boiled down to the point where the ball contacts the racket strings. This book gave me reasons for following-through the ball with my racket and using top spin. Once I understood the reasons, the actions came easily and my game improved dramatically. I finally began to enjoy tennis.

This experience with tennis raised the question of why the same principle couldn't be applied to skiing. Could the sport of skiing be condensed to a single fundamental point upon which skiing technique is built? The answer was yes. All actions in skiing can be focused on one point—the ski. Expanding this idea further, there are only four actions that can be performed on a ski. The ski can be turned onto one of its edges, balanced by shifting weight to different parts of the ski, unweighted by temporarily removing the body's weight from the ski, and rotated by pivoting it under the foot to change direction. These four ways to control a ski may be called the basic skills: edging, balancing, unweighting, and rotating. They provide a framework upon which all skiers can improve their techniques. This is the basis for this book.

The Anatomy of Skiing is not a technical book. Simple language is used to explain the fundamentals of skiing and how they are based on the anatomy of muscles and joints.

The Anatomy of Skiing follows two teaching principles: 1) Emphasize the essential points, then master the details. 2) A skill can be easier to learn, particularly for adults, if you first understand the reasons for your actions. Then, instead of memorizing movements that seem unrelated, you will appreciate how the actions fit together and will then be able to organize them in a logical pattern.

The Anatomy of Skiing differs from other books on skiing because it stresses basic skills. The first part of the book describes these skills and the different ways they are performed. It distinguishes the essential actions from the less important ones. It answers the questions "Why do it this way?" and "Why is this so important?" The second part tells how to combine these basic movements to improve your skiing ability.

The beginner, intermediate, and advanced skier all use the same basic skills, although they apply them in a different way. The novice learns the fundamental actions in their easiest forms. The intermediate develops more ways to perform the basic skills and concentrates on executing them in proper sequence. The advanced skier not only utilizes a variety of actions but also learns to perform them with precision, smoothness, and efficiency of motion.

The first edition of *The Anatomy of Skiing* has been revised by the addition of two new sections. The first is on the principles of cross-country skiing. The second deals with health and safety on the slopes, including information on pre-season conditioning, frostbite, clothing, eye protection, safety equipment, tree skiing, avalanches, and much more. The chapter on first aid provides the non-physician with useful tips on how to evaluate and manage injuries until professional assistance arrives. The material in this section will be helpful to downhill and cross-country skiers, as well as to mountain climbers and others who walk and travel in the high country.

R.J.S.

Part I

The Basic Skills

Summary: Controlling the edges of the skis is the first principle of skiing. Edging is achieved by combining two actions of the knees: bending the knees (flexion) and pushing the knees to the side (knee angulation). Knee angulation, also called cranking, is the main action that controls the edges. However, knee angulation is possible only when the knees are flexed.

A ski is similar to a flat board with two edges. If you lay the ski flat, it will slide downhill, out of control. But press an edge of the ski into the hill, and it will stop. Most skiing is therefore done on the edges of the skis, and many of the body movements in skiing are designed to control the ski's edges.

The ski's edges are controlled by movements of the legs. Since the ski is fixed to the boot, and the boot is fitted snugly to the foot, any action that directs the foot inside or outside will turn the ski onto its inside or outside edge *(Figure 1)*. Ordinarily three joints have the ability to produce an edge change: the ankle, knee, and hip. In skiing, the ankle plays no significant role in edging because the modern ski boot is so stiff and high that the ankle is unable to roll the foot inside or outside. The remaining two joints, the knee and hip, work together to control the ski's edges.

Knee Angulation

The hip joint is capable of movement in all directions. However, the effect of hip motion on the ski's edges depends on whether the knees are straight or bent. With straight knees, the knee joints are locked, rigid, incapable of any motion that will edge the skis. Only the hip joints can move, and their effect on the edges is limited. On the other hand, when the knees are bent (flexed), the knee joints are unlocked. The hips can roll the knees to the side, and the loosened knee joints can rotate the lower legs and feet in the opposite direction.

Bending your knees is the single most important action in skiing. Knee bending is essential because it

Figure 1

Inside and Outside Edges

The inside and outside edges of the skis are controlled by lateral (sideways) movements of the knees. On the left, the skis are set on their inside edges by rolling the knees inward to touch each other. On the right, the skis are set on their outside edges by rolling the knees away from each other. In both actions, there is no ankle motion because the stiff ski boot prevents it.

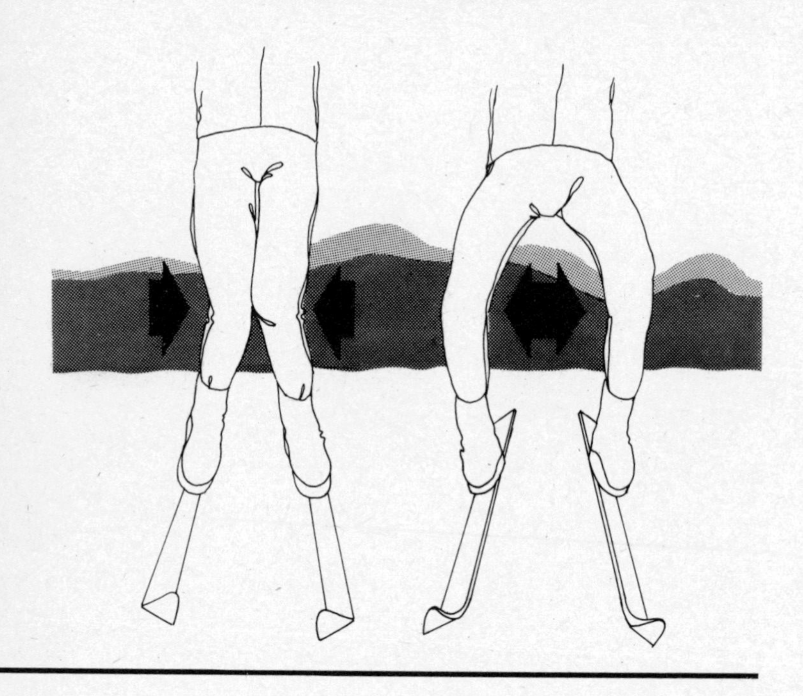

permits your knees to roll sideways, thereby edging your skis. And the more you bend your knees, the greater will be the degree of knee angulation attainable. This, in turn, provides more edge control and increases your ability to turn and stop.

To better understand how the knee and hip joints work together, let's examine the snowplow and parallel positions, first with straight knees, then with flexed knees.

Snowplow with Straight and Flexed Knees

In the snowplow position with straight knees, your hips fix the skis on their inside edges by rotating the toes inward and the heels outward *(Figure 2A)*. However, the degree of edging is limited. On gentle slopes, a snowplow with straight knees can be effective, but on steeper slopes more edging is required. By bending

Straight vs. Flexed Knees

Figures 2A and 2B

2A) The snowplow position with the thighs pushed apart, the toes turned inward, and the heels pushed outward. The knees are straight and the skis lie slightly on their inside edges.

2B) The same position as A with one exception. The knees and ankles are now flexed, permitting the knees to roll inward, almost touching each other. The result is a significant increase in the degree of edgeset by the inside edges of the skis.

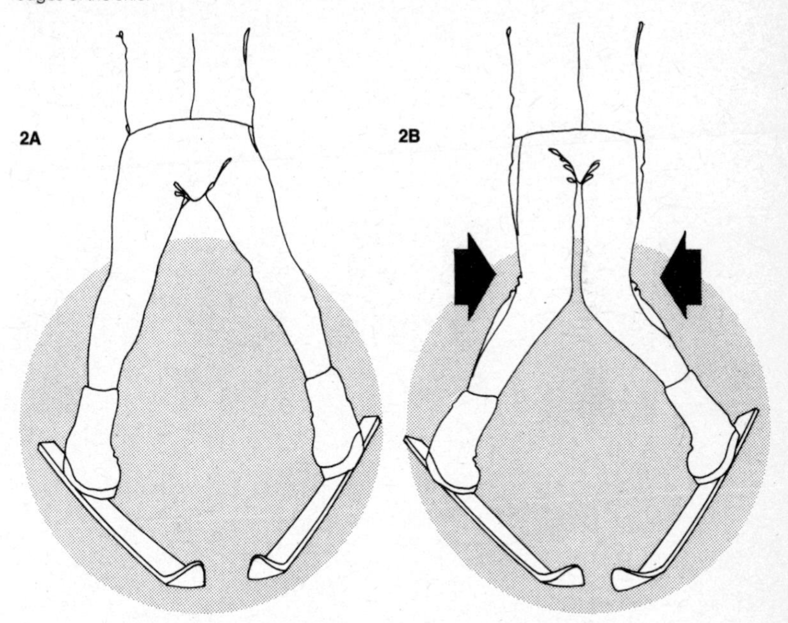

your knees in the snowplow position, the knees can move towards each other, almost touching. (The actual motion is internal rotation of the hip joints.) The result is that both skis have increased their degree of inside edging *(Figure 2B)*.

Parallel Position with Straight and Flexed Knees

In the parallel position with straight knees, your hip joints can set both skis on their uphill edges by pushing your hips uphill *(Figure 3A)*. To maintain balance, your shoulders must lean in the opposite direction, downhill. However, the amount of edging obtained by hip angulation alone is limited. On steep slopes, edging with straight knees is often inadequate. But once your knees are flexed, they can move sideways, resulting in knee angulation and thereby allowing the skis to roll further onto their edges *(Figure 3B)*.

Figure 3

Knee and Hip Angulation

A) Hip Angulation Alone. The hips push uphill and the shoulders drop downhill to set the skis on their uphill edge. The knees are straight. The amount of edging obtainable is limited. **B) Hip and Knee Angulation.** Flexing (bending) the knees unlocks the knee joints, making it possible for the knees to be pushed sideways (knee angulation), along with the hips. The addition of knee angulation permits a much greater degree of edging than hip angulation alone. This has been called the comma position because the body configuration is curved like a comma. **C) Knee Angulation Alone.** The hips and shoulders remain straight. The degree of edging attainable with knee angulation alone is close to that in B, where both knee and hip angulation are combined.

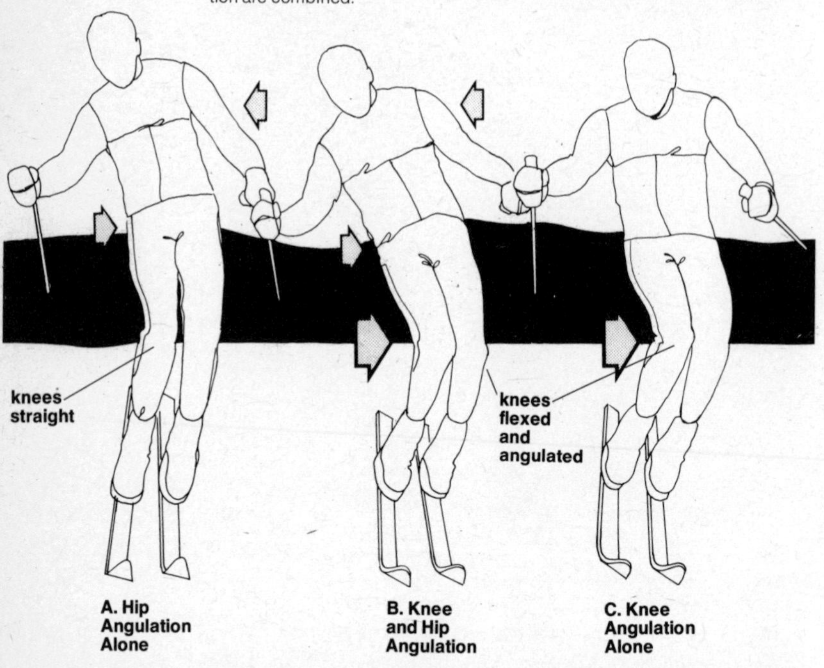

A. Hip Angulation Alone **B. Knee and Hip Angulation** **C. Knee Angulation Alone**

Knee Angulation and Hip Angulation

In the past, ski schools have talked about body angulation of the "comma position." This is described as pushing the knees uphill (knee angulation), pushing the hips uphill (hip angulation), and dropping the shoulders in the opposite direction, downhill *(Figure 3B)*.

Today, most ski schools agree that knee angulation is much more important than hip angulation—so much so that the "comma position" is seldom taught. With good knee angulation the upper half of the body can remain fixed. The hips need not move uphill and the shoulders need not compensate by leaning downhill.

Knee Angulation

Figure 4

The skis are rolled high on their right edges by knee angulation, rolling the knees to the right. Note that the knees are considerably flexed in order to permit this degree of knee angulation. (Copper Mountain photo by Rick Godin.)

Knee angulation can increase edge setting without displacing the body's center of gravity *(Figure 3C and Figure 4).* Although hip angulation assists in edge control, knee angulation does most of the work.

Banking

There is another important technique of edge control —leaning uphill, against centrifugal force, or banking. Because banking cannot be used until you can move with moderate speed, it will be discussed later (Chapter 9). Knee angulation should be mastered before learning to bank, as knee angulation is THE most important method of edge control.

Summary: The proper body stance has two requirements:
1) bending the knees
2) distributing your weight evenly between the heels and balls of the feet for proper balance.

To achieve good balance on skis, knee flexion must be counterbalanced by ankle flexion. Knee flexion alone lowers your seat, placing more weight on your heels. Ankle flexion alone pushes your shins against the boot tops, placing more weight on the toes and balls of your feet. The correct skiing position combines each amount of knee flexion with the appropriate amount of ankle flexion to maintain balance. Advanced skiers may use as much as 90 degrees or more of knee flexion. This cannot be completely counterbalanced by ankle flexion, as the ankles cannot bend that far. Therefore, balance is achieved by bending forward at the waist, enough to maintain equal weight distribution between the balls and heels of the feet.

Once your knees are bent, attention should be focused on your weight, which should be on both feet, with the weight in the "center" of the foot. The term "center of the foot" is confusing because the middle portion of the foot is arched and carries little weight. The heel and the ball are the actual weight-bearing points. One does not "feel" the weight in the center of the foot, but on the heel and the ball of the foot. Thus, the term "centered on the foot" means that the weight is distributed between the heel and the ball.

The reason for centering your weight is stability. By maintaining part of your weight on the heel of your foot and part on the ball, your weight is distributed over a base of 7 to 10 inches—that is, the length of the foot. If your weight was always on a single point (either on the heel or the ball of the foot), balance would be most difficult.

Weight Distribution Between Ball and Heel

While skiing, the weight distribution between heel and ball constantly fluctuates by subtle, small shifts of weight forward and backward. These weight shifts are normal. Occasionally, more weight will be suddenly thrust forward to the balls of the feet, if, for example, you make a sharp turn. But the weight will soon shift back to the "center" of the feet. When skiing in deep powder, it is essential that your weight never advance forward. It should be centered with a little more weight on the heels to keep the ski tips riding out of the snow. However, the increased weight on the heels is minimal because some weight must always remain on the balls of the feet. Although the actual distribution of weight between heel and ball varies under different circumstances, the key factor in maintaining good balance is to always keep some weight on both the heel and the ball of your foot.

Knees Flexed and Weight Centered

The correct body stance in skiing is a posture with bent knees and the weight centered over both feet. The amount of knee flexion may vary from as little as 20 degrees to over 90 degrees. This is because knee bending is necessary not only to permit knee angulation for edging (Chapter 1), but also to lower the body's center of gravity (for stability) and to act as a shock absorber over bumps and moguls. On gentle, flat slopes, less knee flexion is required than on steep or bumpy slopes, where a great deal of knee flexion is often needed. Thus, the correct body stance will vary under different slope conditions. However, in all the variations, your knees must be bent and your weight centered on your feet.

Coordinating Knee, Ankle, and Waist Flexion

The aim of a proper body stance is to provide good balance. This is achieved by coordinating knee bending with flexion of your ankles and waist, permitting your weight to remain centered over your feet. Bending your knees alone throws your body's weight onto your heels. On the other hand, flexing your ankles and your waist forward transfers the weight to the balls of your feet *(Figure 5)*.

Keeping your knees bent and your weight centered is simple: As you bend your knees, keep your balance by bending your ankles forward *(Figure 6A)*. Your ankles are more limited than your knees in their flexion ability. So when your ankles are bent as far as possible, continue to bend your knees and transfer your weight back to your heels *(Figure 6B)*. To recenter the weight on your feet and re-establish good balance, you

Figure 5

Balance — Fore and Aft

The three factors that affect weight distribution between the heels and balls of the feet are knee flexion, ankle flexion, and waist flexion.

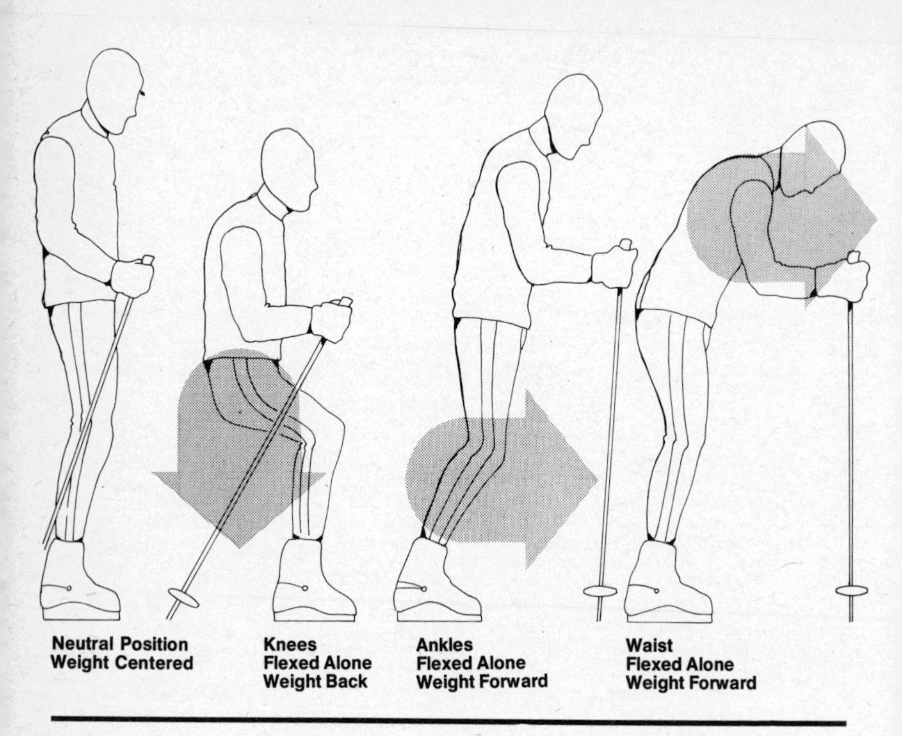

must now bend forward from the waist *(Figure 6C)*.

Your choice of body stance depends on how much knee flexion you want. Increased knee flexion is more difficult to maintain because it puts more strain on the thigh muscles and requires more energy. On the other hand, increased knee flexion permits more knee angulation, and hence greater edge control. On steeper slopes, this is highly desirable.

Leverage: Forward and Backward Weight Transfer

Leverage is shifting your weight to the front or back part of the ski to make the ski perform more efficiently. Leverage is used to assist in turning, checking, stopping, or accelerating.

■ *Forward leverage* is shifting your weight forward to the balls of your feet, taking some weight off your heels. You feel forward leverage as increased pressure of your shins against your boot tops. Forward leverage

Balancing Increased Knee Flexion

Figure 6

Coordinating knee flexion, ankle flexion, and waist flexion maintains a balanced position with the weight centered on the feet. **A)** Knee and ankle flexion are balanced, permitting the weight to be centered. **B)** Increased knee flexion transfers the weight back to the heels. The ankles cannot flex any further forward to counterbalance the knees. **C)** From the unstable position in B, the only way to get more weight forward is to bend at the waist.

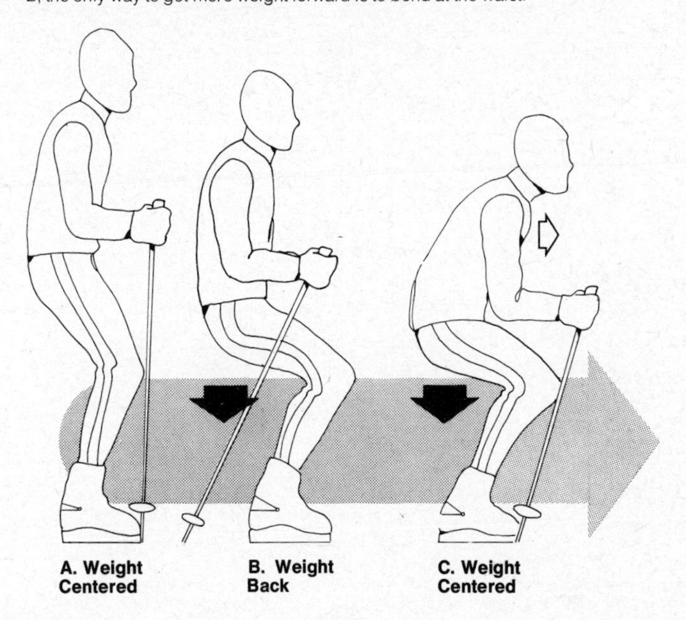

increases the pressure on the ski tips, making them grab the snow. It takes pressure off the tails, permitting them to pivot more easily around the tips. Pressure on the tips also reduces speed.

■ *Backward leverage* is transferring weight back to your heels. It takes pressure off the tips and reverses the effects of forward leverage.

Leverage should be used subtly and gently, not abruptly. Weight should not be transferred completely to either the heels or the balls of the feet. Minimal shifts of weight forward and backward are usually sufficient to produce adequate leverage.

Leverage is more a secondary than a primary tool in skiing. It can be very useful but is not essential. It cannot be used to any extent in deep powder snow because there is not a firm base against which to push the skis.

3 Ski Construction

How It Affects Turning

Skis are designed with the tip and tail wider than the midsection: The resulting curve is called the ski's side camber or side-cut *(Figure 7A)*. When the ski is set on its edge, as in edging, the tip and tail will bite the side of the hill, suspending the midsection or waist in mid-air. Since the body's weight is over the midsection, this part of the ski gives way, producing a curve in the ski *(Figures 7C and 8)*. This curve or arc is used to turn and change direction.

Two factors determine the size of that arc: 1) the flexibility or stiffness of the ski and 2) the weight of the skier. The maximum arc (producing the sharpest turn) is made by a heavy skier on a flexible ski. In contrast, the minimum arc is made by a light skier on a stiff ski.

Anatomy of a Ski

Figure 7

A) The tip and tail of the ski are wider than the midsection (or the waist). This is the ski's side camber or side-cut. **B)** Most skis are built with an arc in the center which is called the ski's camber. **C)** When the tip and tail are suspended and the center of the ski weighted, the camber is reversed.

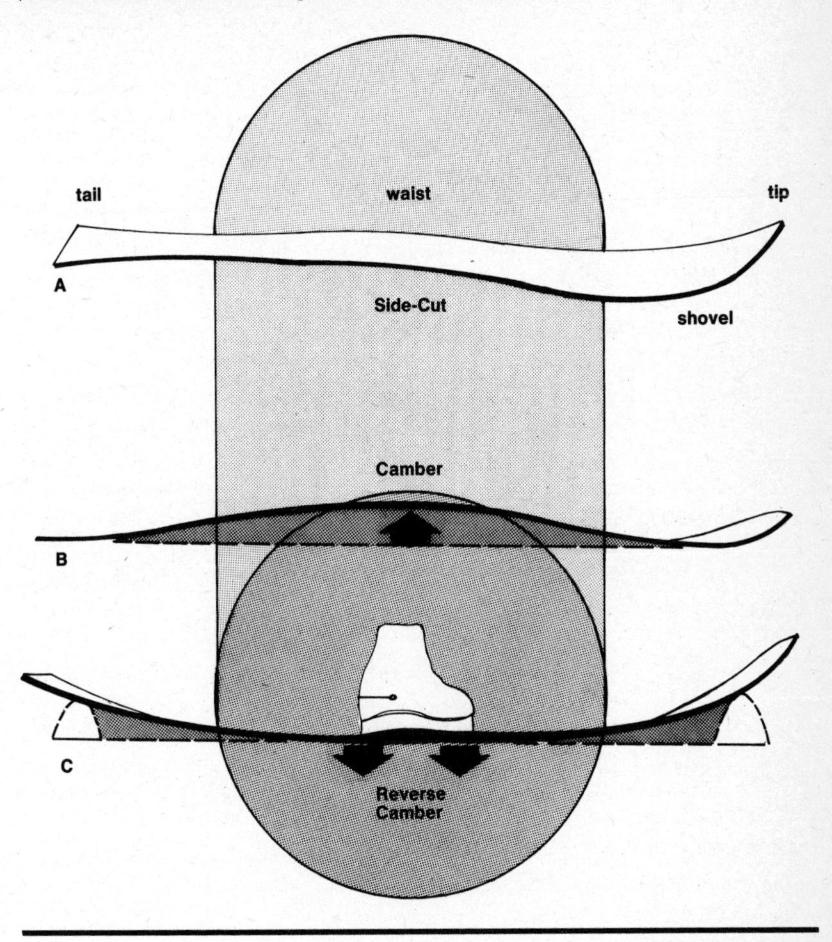

Figure 8

Carving With Reverse Camber

The skis are turned on their edges so that the tips and tails contact the snow. The midsection is suspended until the skier's weight pushes it downward. This reverses the camber of the ski, producing a curve. A turn that follows this curve is a "carved turn," as discussed in Chapter 4.

4 Turning

Summary: Turns are initiated by changing the direction of the skis with either a stem or parallel movement. The stem turn transfers weight to a single ski edge without unweighting. The parallel turn usually requires a moment of unweighting while both skis either rotate together or change their edges.

Turns are completed by either skidding or carving. Skidding is the combination of sideslipping with rotation of the tails of the skis around the tips. Carving is following the direction the ski tips are pointing. In carving there should be no sideslipping and no rotation.

A. Initiation of a turn
1) stem
2) parallel—foot twist or edge change

B. Completion of a turn
1) skidding
2) carving

Initiating a Turn

Initiating a turn means beginning to change the direction of the skis. Once the direction has started to change, the completion phase begins.

■ *Stem turns* are turns initiated by pointing one ski in the new direction, setting it on its inside edge, then transferring the body's weight to that ski. The weight shifts from one foot to the other so that some weight is always on the ground *(Figure 9).* The stem turn is a one-legged turn in which almost all of the weight is transferred to the stemmed ski. Only a minimal amount of weight remains on the other ski.

The origin of teaching skiers to keep all their weight on the turning ski probably comes from the stem turn. Indeed, when stemming, this is a good rule. But this rule should not be applied to parallel turns.

■ *Parallel turns* are turns initiated by changing the direction of both feet together, rather than one at a time

Figure 9

Stem Turn

The stem turn is a one-legged turn performed by transferring the body's weight from one leg to the other. Skiing downhill, the heel is pushed outward and the knee angulated inward to place the stemmed ski on its inside edge, facing in the new direction. Then the hips shift the weight to the stemmed ski. Unweighting both feet is not necessary in stem turns.

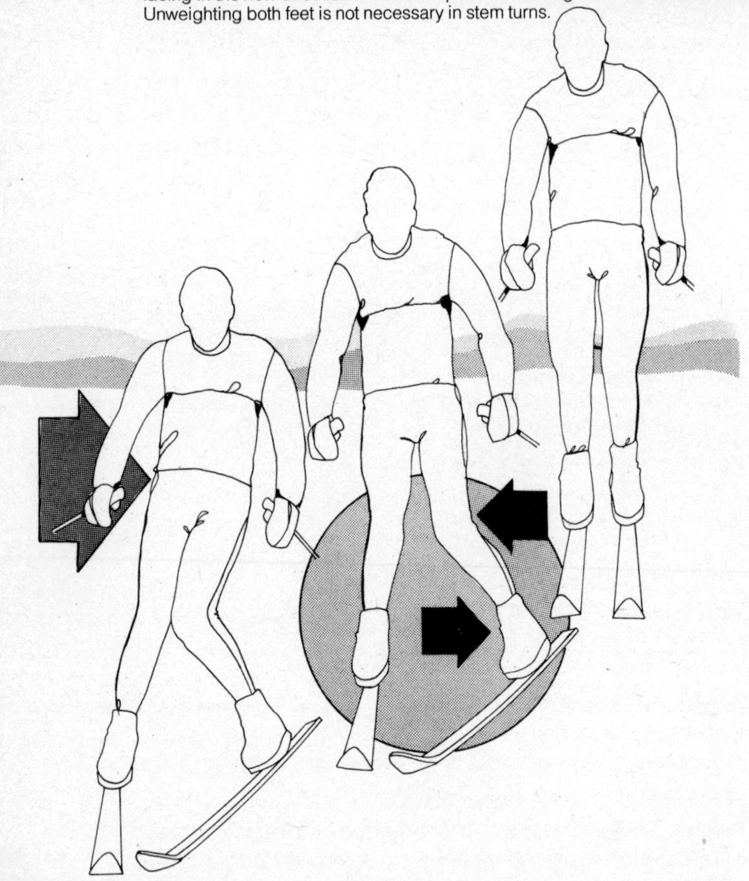

as in stem turns. In order to turn the two feet simultaneously, it is usually necessary to have a moment when the body's weight is off the ground. This is called the moment of "unweighting." It is achieved by a quick hop upwards, a quick bend of the knees to drop the seat downwards, or by skiing over rough terrain (Chapter 5).

Parallel turning can be performed by either rotation, edge change, or both. Rotation is the twisting of the feet, hips, or shoulders in the direction of the turn

Foot Twist

Figure 10

Rotation is used to initiate a parallel turn. While the feet, hips, or shoulders can rotate in the direction of the turn, it is best to rotate the feet (foot twist or foot swivel), rather than the upper body. If the feet are unweighted just before rotation, foot twist is much easier to perform.

(Figure 10). Changing the skis' edges is accomplished by rolling the knees from one side to the other *(Figure 11).* This reverses the arc of the skis, which now bend and curve in the opposite direction. Rotation and edge change may be used in the same turn, but each separately can change the direction of the skis. In general, changing edges is the smoother but slower way to turn. Rotation is necessary for sharper and quicker turns.

In parallel turns, it is not necessary to shift the body's weight from one foot to the other, as is done in stem turns. The weight can remain on both feet throughout the turn.

Completion of a Turn

Once the direction of the skis has changed, the last phase of the turning action commences. Turns are completed by either carving or skidding. Both actions use the same basic mechanism: edgeset. The differ-

Figure 11

Edge Change

Edge change can initiate a parallel turn. By rolling the knees from one side to the other, the edges of the skis will change, as will the direction of the arc in the skis. Unweighting facilitates edge change.

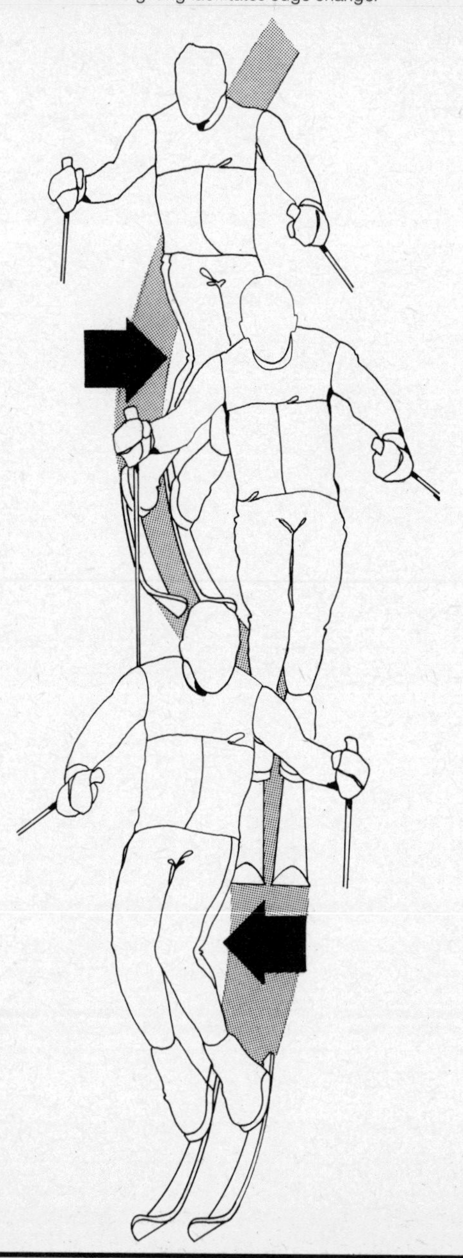

Sideslipping

Figure 12

Sideslipping is moving downhill with the side of the ski leading the way. The edges of the skis are partially flattened against the slope to initiate sliding down the hill. The slide is checked (stopped) by increasing the degree of edgeset into the hill. The prime movers of the skis' edges are the knees. The knees roll downhill to begin sideslipping and roll uphill to check it.

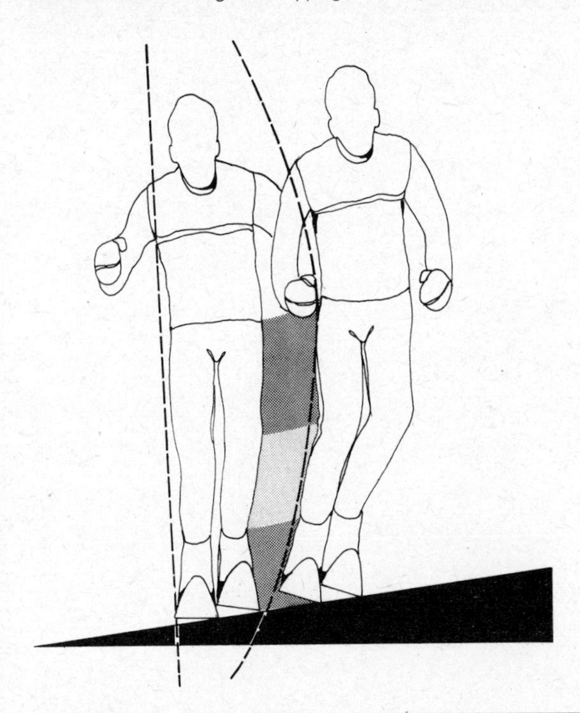

ence between the two is the degree of edgeset and the distribution of weight between the ball and heel of the foot.

An understanding of carving and skidding begins with sideslipping. *Sideslipping* is moving sideways down a slope with the skis perpendicular to the fall line. Sideslipping is controlled by movement of the flexed knees toward and away from the hill *(Figure 12).*

■ *Skidding* is sideslipping combined with rotating the tails of the skis around the tips *(Figure 13).* This can be accomplished by transferring weight forward to the balls of the feet after the turn has begun (called forward leverage). The amount of forward leverage adjusts the arc of the skidded turn. Short radius or sharp turns, with a small arc, are made by transferring con-

Figure 13

Skidding

Skidding is sideslipping combined with rotation of the tails around the tips of the skis. The path of the ski is shown here. The side of the ski leads the way through the turn. Skidding is produced by enough flattening of the edges of the skis to permit sideslipping.

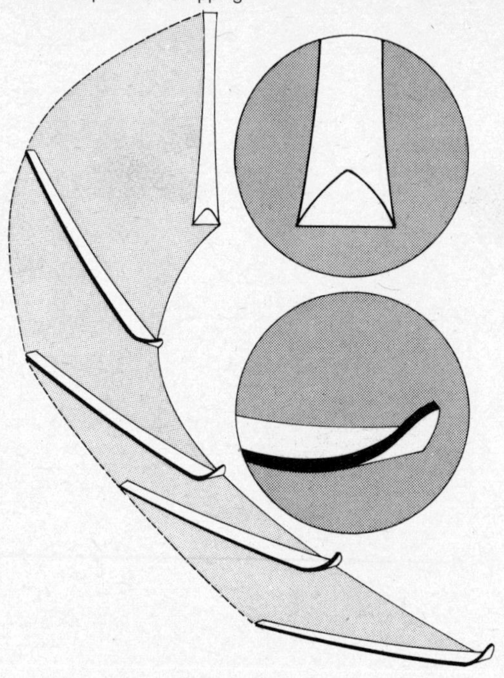

siderable weight forward. Long radius or gradual turns, with wider arcs, are performed with less forward leverage. The more weight remaining on the heels during a skidded turn, the slower the turn and the more gradual the arc.

It is also possible to perform a skidded turn without any forward leverage. In this case, the weight remains equally distributed between the heels and balls of the feet throughout the turn. Here, the turning action is the continuation of the initial turning force whose momentum continues to rotate the skis as long as they lie flat enough to slideslip. When the skier slows down or increases edging to stop slipping, the rotation will stop.

It is difficult, and often impossible, to skid in deep powder because the snow offers too much resistance to sideslipping. For this reason, skidded turns are generally limited to hard-packed slopes. Indeed, the

Carving

Figure 14

Carving is following the direction the skis are pointing. Carving is produced by edging the skis far enough to prevent sideslipping. The tips of the skis lead the way through a carved turn. Both the tips and tails must bear some weight when carving.

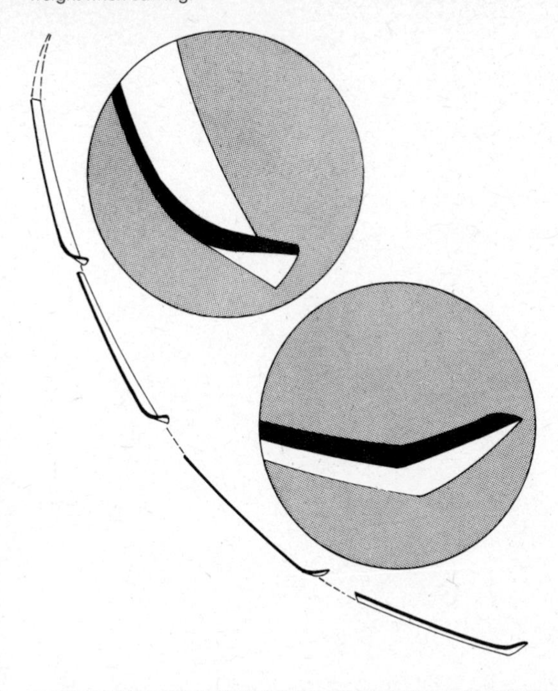

most common reason for having trouble skiing in deep powder is trying to finish turns by skidding. Skidding in powder is effective only when the powder is very light and not too deep (see Chapter 10). The solution to turning in deep powder is carving.

■ *Carving* is traveling in the direction the skis are pointing without slipping to the side. When the skis are edged, the line of the skis' direction will be curved, due to the reversed camber and flexibility of the skis (Chapter 3). The carved turn is, therefore, a turn that follows the arc of the edged ski *(Figure 14)*. It can be initiated by either a stem or a parallel movement. Carving a turn differs from skidding in two ways. First, carving requires a greater degree of edging than skidding. To skid, the edges must lie flat enough against the hill to *permit* slipping, while in carving, the edgeset must increase enough to *prevent* slipping. Second, in skid-

Figure 15

Skidding Initiated by Edge Change or Foot Twist

A turn completed by skidding can begin with edge change or foot twist. Edge change is a smoother, gentler initiation, while foot twist produces a sharper turn with a smaller radius.

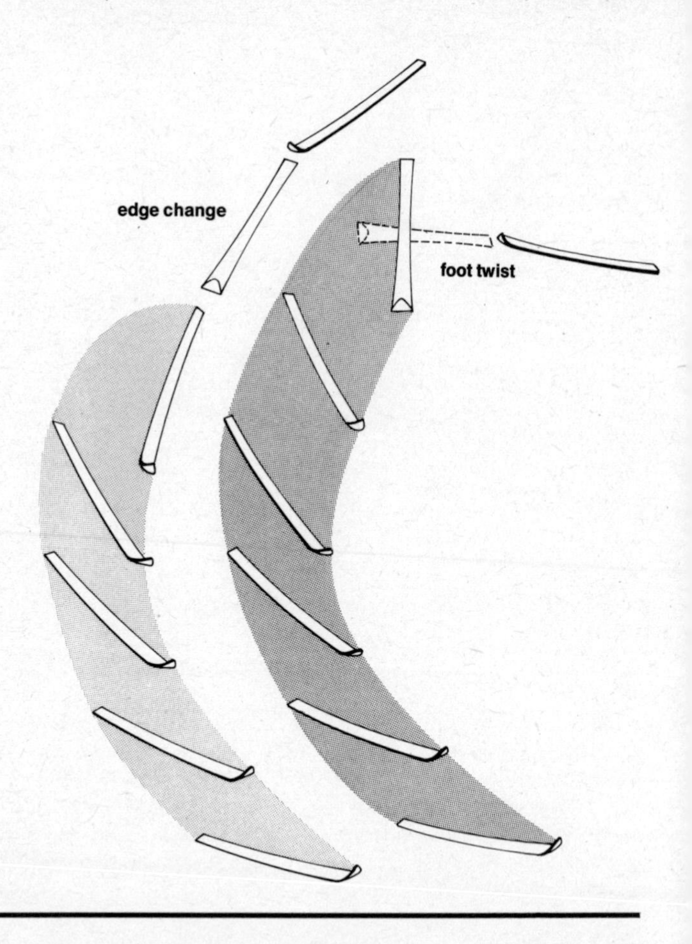

ding, the skis change direction by rotation of the tails around the tips. In carving, there is no rotation. The tails do not rotate around the tips.

Technically, all combinations of initiating and completing turns are possible. A turn completed by skidding can be started by a stem movement, foot twist, or edge change *(Figure 15)*. Carved turns may similarly be initiated by a stem or parallel movement. Changing edges and carving produce a smooth, graceful turn,

Carving Initiated by Edge Change or Foot Twist

Figure 16

A carved turn may begin with edge change or foot twist. Edge change followed by carving produces the "pure" carved turn. It is a gradual, gentle turn. Initiating a turn by foot twist and completing it by carving produces a quicker, sharper turn.

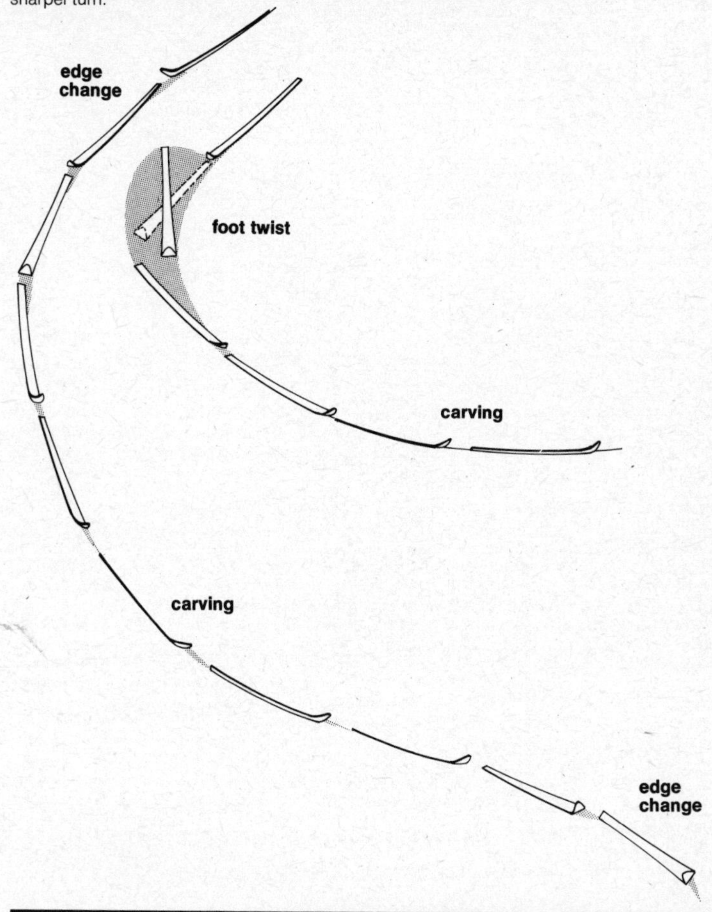

which may be described as the "pure" carved turn. By combining foot twist with carving, a sharper turn results *(Figure 16).* This combination is probably the one most frequently used by good skiers. The foot twist does most of the turning while carving provides the skier with better control and balance before initiating the next turn.

5 Unweighting

Summary: Unweighting is the sudden removal of body weight from both feet. It permits both feet to turn simultaneously, in a new direction. Most parallel turns begin with unweighting. The 4 ways to unweight are:

1. Up-unweighting—with a down-UP motion. This is a quick lift up and should be done without straightening the knees.

2. Down-unweighting—with a simple DOWN motion. This is a quick knee bend, dropping the seat.

3. Leg retraction—is lifting the weight of the feet upwards by simultaneously tightening the abdominal muscles and lifting the knees.

4. Skiing over a bump, mogul, or rough terrain.

Up-Unweighting

Up-unweighting is the most common form of unweighting. It is a sudden lift or hop upwards, raising the seat. Your weight is momentarily suspended in air. In that instant, you feel no weight on your feet.

Up-unweighting is often described as a *down-UP* movement, even though the UP-motion is the only portion that does the unweighting. The preparatory down motion is a vital part of up-unweighting because it permits *your knees to remain flexed at all times during the UP motion.* In order to lift the weight with an UP movement without straightening your knees, you must increase knee flexion just prior to lifting up. This is done by lowering your seat in a down motion. The down motion is followed immediately by the UP motion, which should only partially straighten your knees *(Figure 17).* The result is that you take the weight off your feet for just a moment without changing the position of your body. At the moment of unweighting, your knees are flexed and ready to rotate or change edges.

One of the most common errors in up-unweighting is straightening the knees on the UP movement. This makes it more difficult to rotate the feet and impossible

Up-Unweighting

Figure 17

From an upright position with the knees slightly flexed, knee flexion is increased by dropping the seat down, over the heels (down motion). Plant the pole after the down-motion. This signals the UP motion, which should be quick.

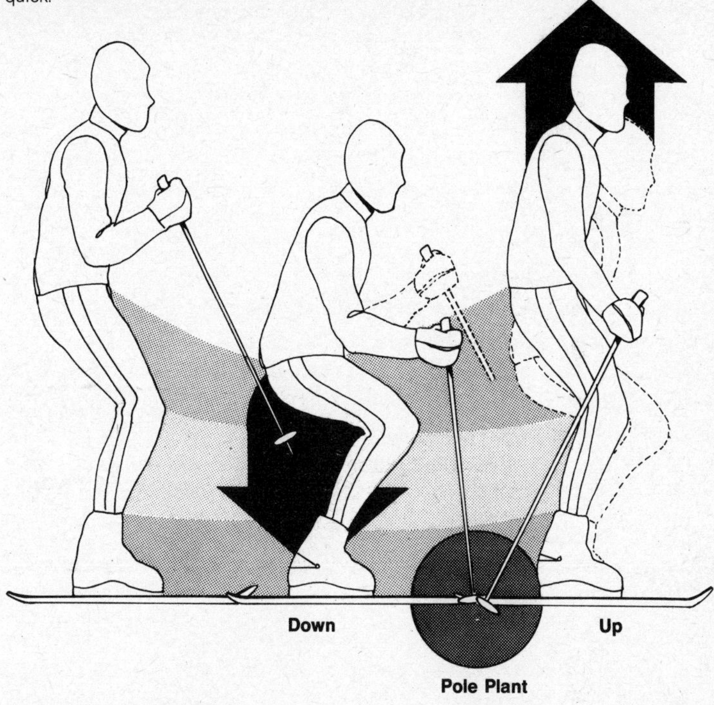

to reset the edges quickly.

The key points in up-unweighting are: 1) speed—the UP motion must be very quick; 2) short displacement—the seat need not drop or lift more than three or four inches; and 3) knees flexed—the knees should never straighten.

Up-unweighting is sometimes described as *"down-UP-down."* However, the addition of the final down motion is not a part of up-unweighting. If the turn is begun during the UP motion, it is often near completion before the final down motion. Thus, the second down motion will be both the final movement of one turn and the preparation for the next. But if you do not turn far enough during the UP motion, you can remedy the situation by dropping your weight down quickly after the UP motion, and thereby perform down-unweighting. During that instant, you can twist your feet further and reset your edges to complete the turn. When this is done, the turn can indeed be described as "down-UP-down." However, only the down-UP portion is part of up-unweighting; the final "down" is actually down-unweighting.

The advantages of up-unweighting are that it is a more familiar movement than down-unweighting—it is similar to jumping up. Up-unweighting permits a more erect position, which is easier and requires less energy than the down position. Up-unweighting is a slower movement, requiring at least one-half second, compared to one-tenth second for down-unweighting. The slower movement provides more time for turning.

Down-Unweighting

Down-unweighting is performed by a quick down movement without a preparatory motion. This is very much like that quick bend of the knee that happens when you are walking barefoot on the beach and step on a sharp stone. Your knee drops quickly to take the weight off your foot. Down-unweighting is the same type of *sudden* drop, using both knees. It may also be described as a quick lowering of the seat *(Figure 18)*. After the turn has started, slowly return your knees to their previous position by raising your seat or extending (straightening) your legs from their acutely flexed position.

The chief advantage of down-unweighting is that at the "moment of truth"—that is, at the moment your feet are "weightless"—your body's position is ideal for turning and edge control because:

1) Knee flexion is at its greatest, thereby permitting maximum knee angulation and edging.

2) The center of gravity is lowest, providing maximum stability, particularly with increased knee angulation.

3) Completion of the turn is easier, since the final movement of a down-unweighted turn is slow extension of the legs. This increases the pressure of the skis against the snow, making edging more effective.

Down-unweighting can be practiced at home, on a bathroom scale. Standing upright on the scale, quickly bend your knees forward and drop your seat. The weight on the scale will suddenly decrease, due to unweighting. The speed of down-unweighting determines how the unweighting occurs. A slow descent

Down-Unweighting

Figure 18

From an upright position, the pole is planted and the seat dropped down suddenly. To be effective, the down motion must be fast.

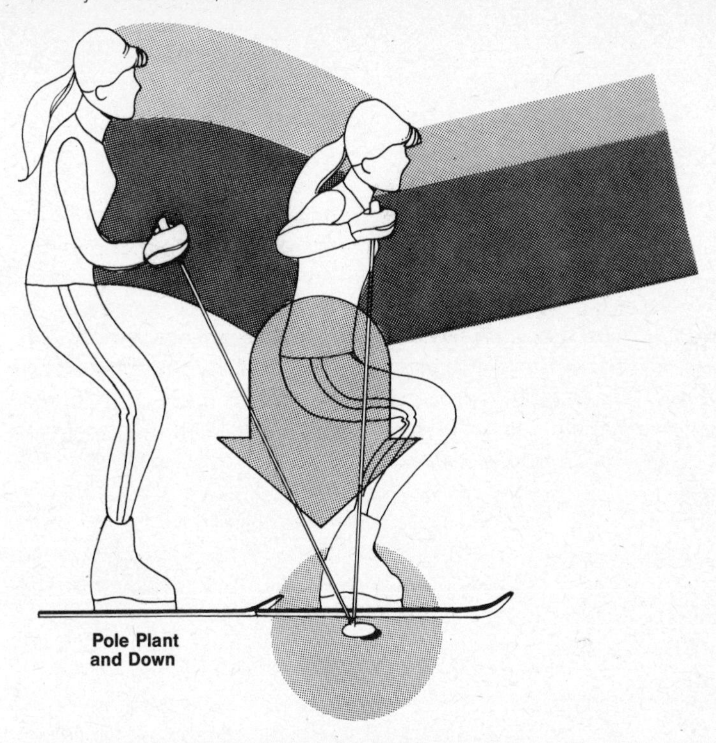

will unweight minimally over a prolonged time. A rapid drop will unweight the feet to a greater extent, but for a shorter time.

Leg Retraction

Leg retraction is lifting the *weight* of the legs up off the ground, without lifting the *feet* off the ground. Thus, it can be regarded as a type of up-unweighting. Like up-unweighting, leg retraction is often preceded by a down motion, so it too can be described as having a down-up rhythm. However, in up-unweighting, the upper body is pushed up by the legs, while in leg retraction, the legs are lifted by the upper body. In up-unweighting the legs do all the work; in leg retraction, the abdominal and back muscles also must work. It takes much less energy for the leg and thigh muscles to push up than for the upper body muscles to lift up.

Figure 19

Leg Retraction

First, a preparatory down motion flexes the knees and lowers the seat. Then unweighting is performed by simultaneously tightening the abdominal muscles and pulling the knees upward. The upper body bends slightly forward at the waist.

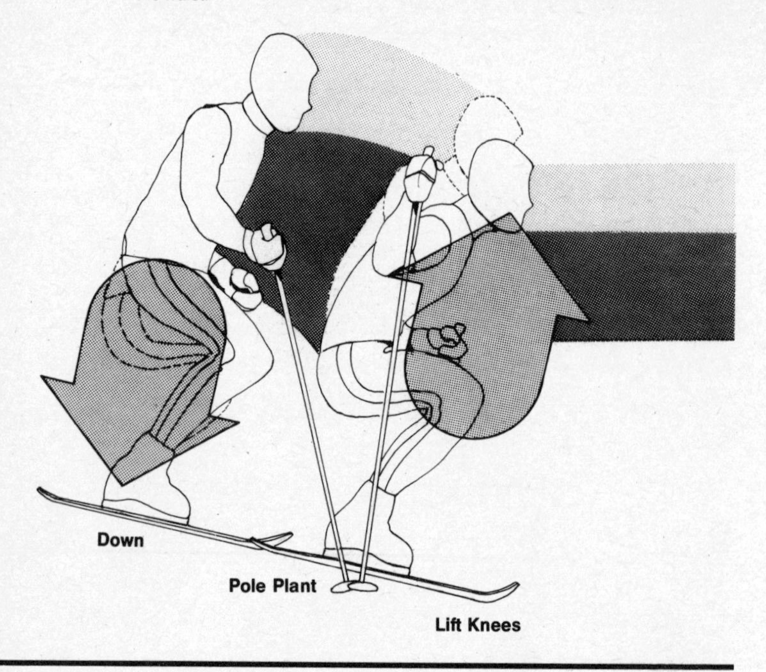

Thus, leg retraction is more demanding and tiring than up-unweighting.

Leg retraction, like up-unweighting, is frequently preceded by a preparatory down motion. But leg retraction should not be confused with down-unweighting. The two are quite different. In down-unweighting, the moment of unweighting occurs *while* the seat is dropping down. In contrast, leg retraction unweights the feet *after* the seat is down. The muscle action is also different. In down-unweighting the seat is lowered by relaxing the thigh muscles, so the work is done by gravity. With leg retraction, the body must do more work to lift the legs against the pull of gravity. Leg retraction is performed by tightening the abdominal and the hip flexor muscles.* The abdominal muscles,

**The strongest hip flexors are the iliopsoas muscles. These muscles run from the lower spinal bones (lumbar vertebrae) to the thigh bones (femurs). The rectus femoris muscle is another hip flexor* (Figure 20).

Muscles of Leg Retraction

Figure 20

A) The muscles that retract the legs are the thigh flexors. The iliacus and psoas muscles attach to the femur together, in a single tendon. The rectus femoris is a weaker muscle. **B)** With the leg and thigh straight, the thigh flexors must do more work. **C)** With the hip flexed 90°, the muscles that flex the thigh have a better mechanical advantage. However, the iliopsoas is still pivoting a bone 14 to 18 inches long by pulling only 4 or 5 inches from the hinge. This is why leg retraction requires more strength and energy than other types of unweighting.

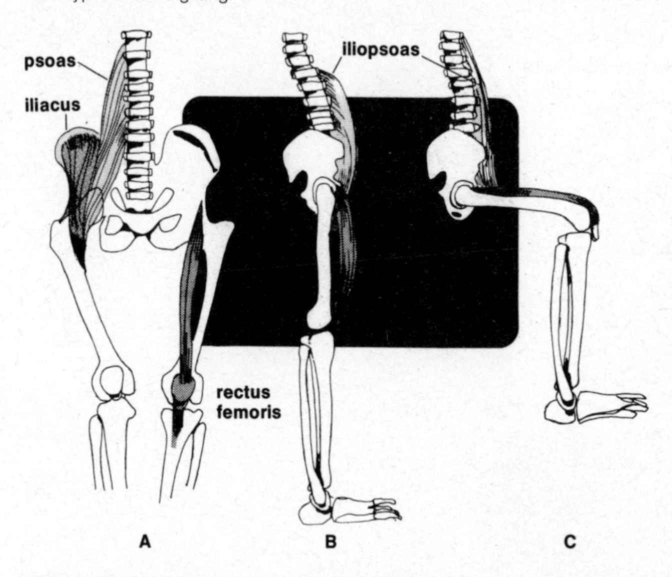

with the aid of a pole plant, steady the upper body while the hip flexors lift the legs *(Figure 19).*

Leg retraction can be performed from any degree of flexion, but it is more efficient when the knees and thighs are deeply flexed, close to 90 degrees. In this position, the hip flexors have a better mechanical advantage from which to lift the knees *(Figure 20).*

Leg retraction is usually accompanied by flexion at the waist because lifting the thighs from a flexed position transfers the body's weight backward. There are two reasons for this. First, lifting the legs up from a flexed position rotates the upper body backwards, around an axis running through the hips *(Figure 21).* Second, the muscles which extend the legs (the quadriceps) are stretched when the knees are flexed *(Figure 22).* Lifting the knees stretches them even further. Thus, when the feet are unweighted, the stretched leg extensors shorten. In doing so they advance the lower

Figure 21

Leg Retraction Rotates Weight Backwards

Leg retraction rotates the body's weight backwards on an axis through the hips. To counteract this force, the upper body leans forward at the waist.

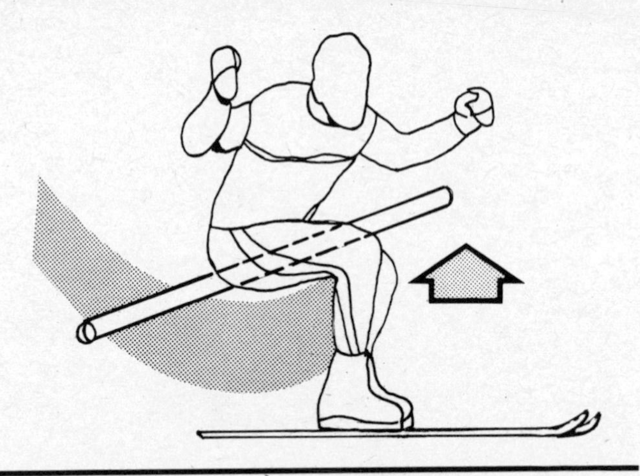

Figure 22

Stretched Extensor Muscles

Leg retraction puts additional stretch on the extensor muscles of the legs (quadriceps). Unweighting the feet releases the stretched muscles, resulting in the feet jetting forward.

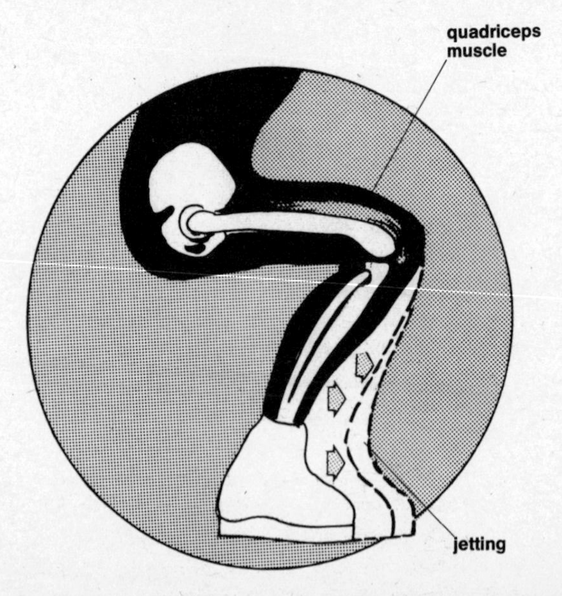

Leg Retracting

Figure 23

You can feel leg retraction by suspending yourself between two chairs and holding your arms straight. Lifting your knees up is similar to leg retraction.

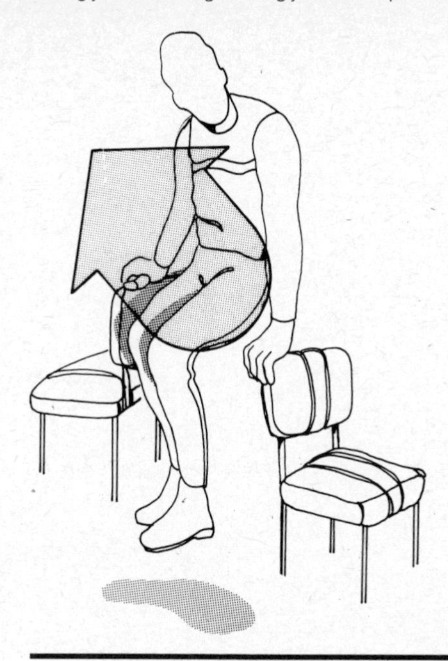

legs and feet, producing the "jetting" of the feet forward that is characteristic of jet-turns and avalement. The feet moving forward transfer the skier's weight backwards. In order to counterbalance these backward forces, the upper body leans forward at the waist as the legs are retracted *(Figure 19)*. This keeps the weight centered over the feet.

To practice leg retraction suspend yourself between the backs of two chairs. With your arms straight, pull your knees upward. You are leg retracting *(Figure 23)*.

Leg retraction is used on rough terrain and moguls, particularly at moderate and high speeds. It can also be used on flat slopes to provide quick turns. (See Chapters 21 and 22.)

Skiing over Rough Terrain

The fourth form of unweighting is the easiest. Skiing over a mogul leaves your feet momentarily weightless at the instant your feet pass the crest of the mogul *(Figure 24)*. At that moment, your feet can twist and the

Figure 24

Unweighting on a Mogul

On a mogul, the tips and tails of the skis are suspended in air and are free to pivot. Just beyond the crest, the downside of the mogul will move away from the skis, thereby unweighting them too.

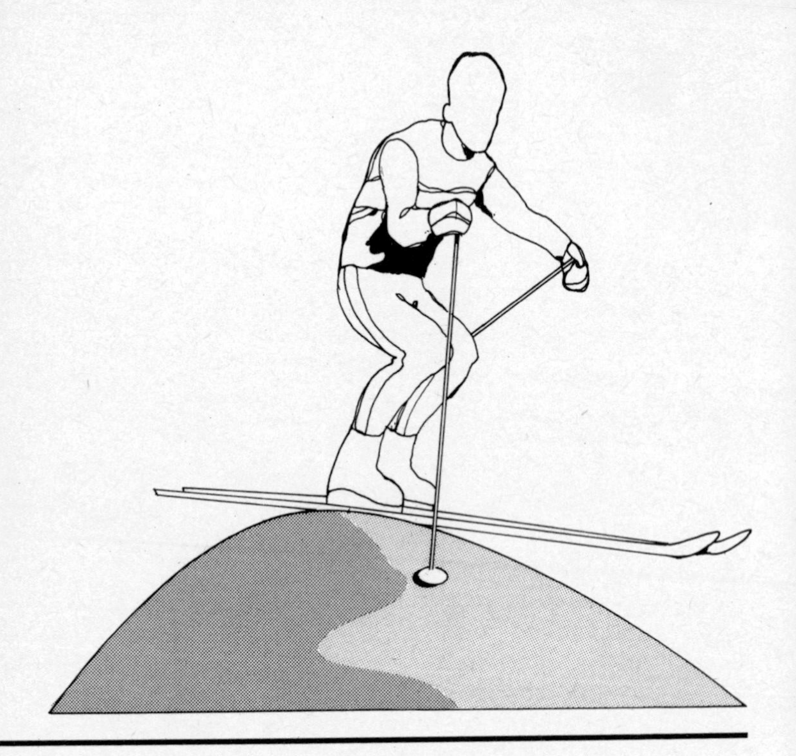

edges of the skis can be reset without further efforts to unweight, either up or down. Turning on the tip of a mogul is easy because you are suddenly suspended in air. Your weight is not yet supported by the downside of the mogul and the tips and tails of your skis are floating, offering minimal resistance to pivoting.

Ski Poles

The use of the ski poles will be discussed more fully in Chapter 8. However, planting the downhill ski pole to assist unweighting should be mentioned at this point. Just prior to unweighting, by any method, place your downhill pole in the snow to the side of the downhill ski. By pushing down on this pole, a small amount of your weight can be lifted from your feet.

6 Rotation

Summary: Rotation is one of the main turning forces. The feet and shoulders are the main rotators in skiing. The hips may also aid, but this is not desirable. Foot rotation is a twisting of the feet during the moment of unweighting. Shoulder rotation can be performed before turning (anticipation) or during the turn. The most efficient way to turn quickly and continuously is to maintain the upper body facing downhill; the lower body pivots to one side, then the other, with each turn.

As mentioned in Chapter 4, two turning forces can change the direction of the skis: edging the skis, to follow the arc of the skis, and rotation, movement around the long axis of the body.

Picture a person standing straight, with a long flagpole running from the head to a point between the two feet *(Figure 25).* Throwing one shoulder forward and the other backward will turn the body around the flagpole in a circle. This circular movement about a central axis is rotation.

Four parts of the body may rotate in skiing: the feet, knees, hips, and shoulders. The most important of these are the feet and shoulders.

Foot Rotation

Foot rotation is often called foot twist, swivel, or pivot. The feet rotate by action of the lower leg muscles. However, when standing on skis, foot rotation is very difficult unless the feet are unweighted. Riding on a chair lift is an excellent way to feel the action of foot twist. Here, the feet are completely unweighted and can be twisted in either direction without moving the knees or hips *(Figure 26).* On the lift, you can observe that foot rotation is limited to about 15 degrees. When more turning is required, foot rotation is combined with other forms of rotation.

Figure 25

Rotating on Body's Long Axis

Rotation is pivoting the body around its long axis, which runs from the center of the head to between the feet. Rotation can be performed by the arms, hips, knees, or feet.

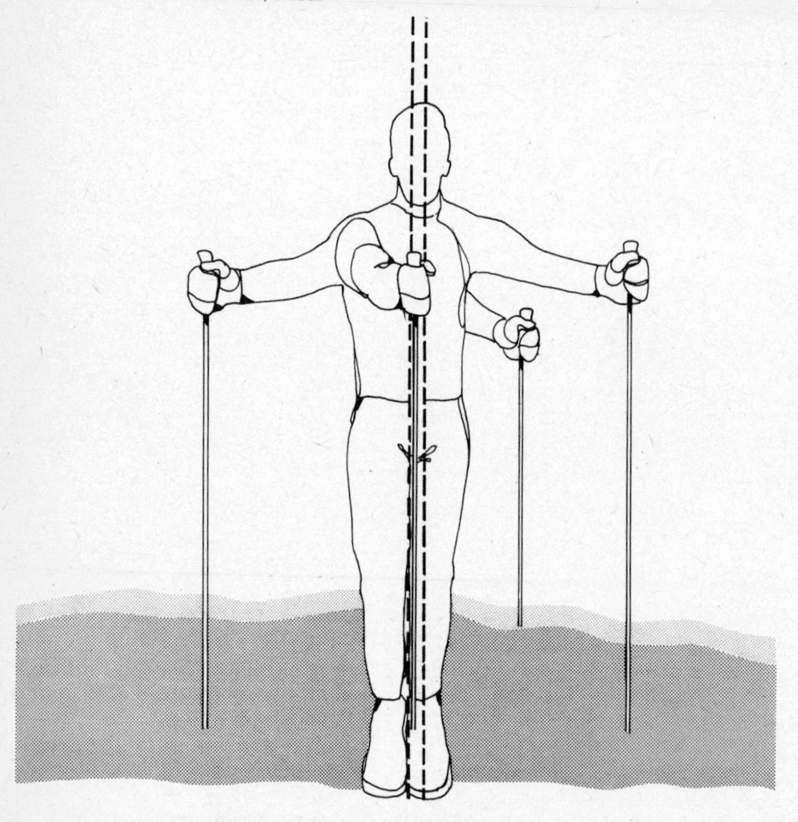

Shoulder Rotation

Some form of shoulder rotation is used in most turns. While your feet can pivot only when they are unweighted, your shoulders can rotate any time during the turn and can even rotate before the turn.

Anticipation

Rotating your shoulders downhill before the skis begin to turn is called anticipation because the upper body is looking ahead, anticipating the direction of the next turn. Anticipation can be performed long before the turn begins. By rotating your shoulders downhill, you stretch the muscles that connect your thighs to your upper body (abdominal and back muscles). This

Foot Twist While Unweighted

Figure 26

Foot rotation can be felt and observed while riding a chair lift. With the hands resting above the knees, the feet can be twisted from side to side without moving the knees or thighs. This is the same muscle action that is used in foot twist.

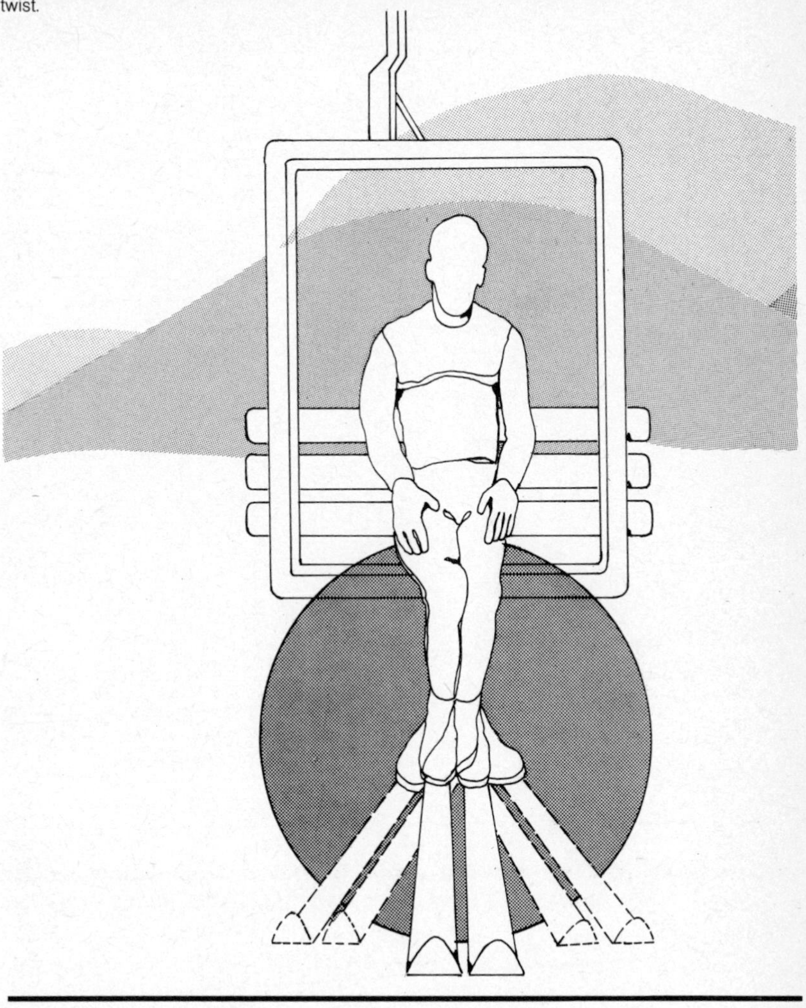

is similar to stretching a rubber band between two points. When your legs are unweighted, your muscles shorten automatically, twisting your feet downhill. Your feet now point in the same direction as your upper body, which remained fixed. This muscle action is similar to the shortening of the stretched rubber band when one end is released *(Figure 27).*

Figure 27

Anticipation

Anticipation is turning the head, shoulders, and arms downhill before the feet turn. This stretches the abdominal and back muscles. At the moment of unweighting, the stretched muscles shorten, pulling the feet around automatically, to face in the same direction as the upper body.

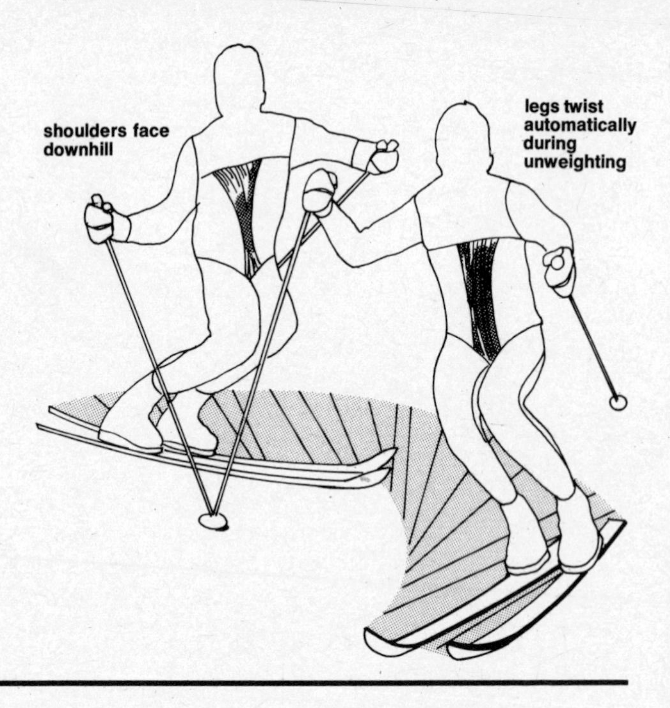

The Shoulders During Completion of the Turn

Once the upper and lower halves of your body are both facing downhill, the rotation forces of the turn are near completion. The skies are then directed back uphill by either skidding or carving, actions that require only the legs and thighs. The upper half of the body can:

1) remain facing downhill

2) passively follow the lower half by keeping the shoulders "square to the skis" (facing the ski tips)

3) forcefully rotate uphill—adding extra shoulder rotation for a very sharp turn.

■ *Remain facing downhill.* When making turns in rapid succession, it is best to keep your head and shoulders facing downhill throughout the turn. As your legs continue to rotate the skis across the hill, your upper body remains stable. As a result, your abdominal muscles are again stretched. Once again your body is in position to anticipate the next turn. Note that the position was assumed by rotating the lower half of your body instead of the upper half. However, the result is the same regardless of which half performed the movement. By keeping the upper body always facing downhill, turns are performed in the most efficient way and in the least amount of time.

■ *Following the lower half.* It is not necessary to always keep the upper body facing downhill. This is required only when making fast, linked turns. When turning slowly and when traversing a hill, there is no reason to twist your upper body to face downhill while your skis and lower half face across the hill. Your upper body will be more comfortable, and less strained, if it simply faces the tips of the skis. Your shoulders will be "square" to the hips and skis. Just prior to the next turn, your shoulders should again rotate to face downhill, in the position of anticipation. In this case, the shoulders have enough time to anticipate; there is no urgency.

■ *Forcefully rotate uphill.* It is possible for your shoulders to rotate uphill ahead of your lower body. This is usually a move of desperation, when you are losing control and can't turn or stop quickly enough. Rotating your shoulders uphill as the turn progresses is the fastest way of turning the skis uphill to slow them down. However, at the end of the turn your body is facing uphill and will require more time to turn again.

Hip Rotation

Hip rotation is used as an additional turning mechanism to supplement foot rotation and anticipation when stronger rotational forces are needed. A small degree of hip rotation passively accompanies anticipation, although hip rotation should not be regarded as a basic element of anticipation.

Hip rotation is usually reserved for deep powder and difficult, crust snow conditions. It can be accentuated by lifting the outside hip during up-unweighting, to bring the skis closer to the surface of the snow. Lifting the outside hip tilts the pelvis, moving the hips laterally, away from the center of the turn. (It is the reverse of hip angulation.) This type of hip rotation is called hip projection because the hip is thrown outside, giving it a wider rotating arc in which to generate more turning power *(Figure 28).* Hip projection flattens the skis

Figure 28

Hip Projection

Hip projection is rotating the hips while simultaneously lifting the outside hip. This de-angulates the hips, flattens the skis, and makes it easier for the skis to rotate. It also gives the hips more turning power because they can swing in a wider arc.

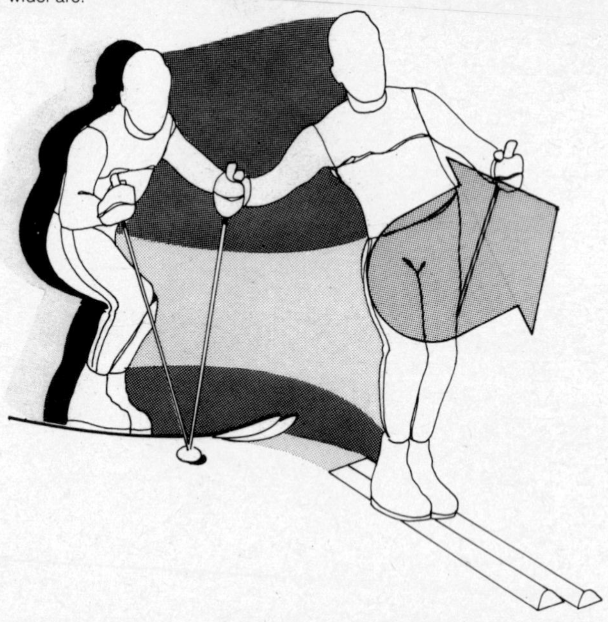

against the slope, eliminating edging. This permits the skis to pivot more easily, but it also prevents edge control. Therefore, it is very important that hip projection be used only to initiate the turn. Stop hip projection by leaning the hips inward, toward the center of the turn (called "blocking"). This is essential to permit knee and hip angulation to edge the skis and complete the turn.

Knee Rotation

The knees act primarily as hinge joints with movement in a forward and backward direction only. When the knees are straight (extended), they cannot twist. But when they are flexed, the knee joints are capable of some rotation. Knee angulation and foot twist each utilize a small amount of knee rotation, when the knees are flexed.

Steering

Steering was first described by G. Joubert and J. Vuarnet (*How to Ski the New French Way,* New York:

Steering

Figure 29

Steering is a combination of foot and lower leg rotation with knee angulation. This is an extremely important method of executing small changes in direction without unweighting. It combines the basic elements of skidding and carving.

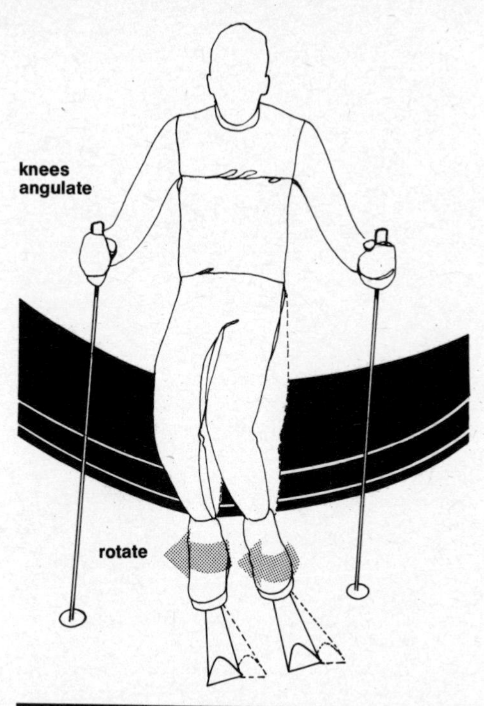

Dial Press, 1967). It is guiding the direction of the skis by a combination of knee angulation (edging) and lower leg rotation. It produces gentle changes in direction without unweighting or weight shifting. It can be used to assist in completing a turn, or it can provide a small, long-radius turn by itself.

Steering is performed with the knees flexed. The knees are pushed inward, in the direction of the turn, to edge the skis. Simultaneously, the leg muscles try to twist the feet in the same direction *(Figure 29).* Because the feet are weighted, they will not pivot or turn quickly, but they will turn gradually. Thus, these forces will gently turn the skis by a combination of carving and skidding. Steering is usually performed by both legs simultaneously, but can be executed by one leg too.

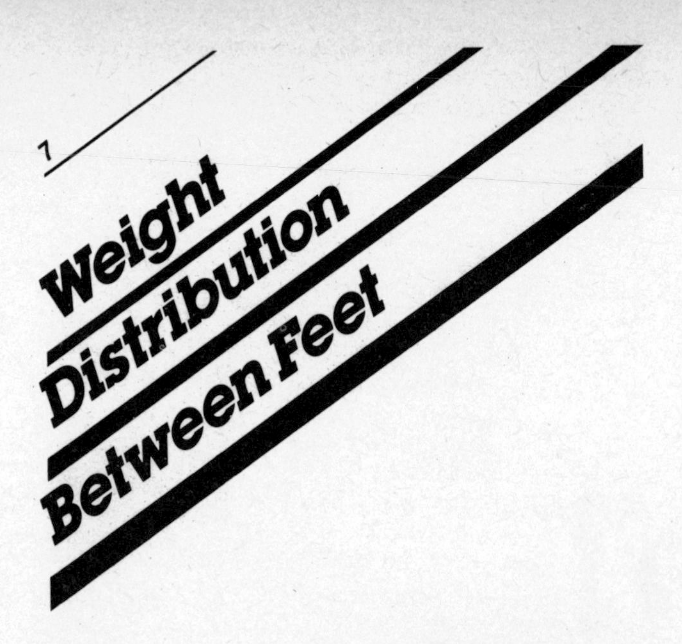

Summary: In the basic stance, some weight is carried on each foot. However, the amount of weight on each foot will vary, since the body maintains its balance by frequent small weight shifts from foot to foot. Weighting both feet provides better balance and more stability in powder and on packed slopes, and helps prevent the ski tips from crossing. More weight on one ski is necessary in stem turns but unnecessary in parallel turns. In parallel turns, both skis should be weighted, although they need not be weighted equally. Frequently more weight is on the outside ski, but there are times when carrying more weight on the inside ski is helpful.

Definitions of Downhill, Uphill, Inside, and Outside Skis

Standing sideways with the skis facing across the hill, the ski closest to the bottom of the hill is the downhill ski, the other one is the uphill ski. While turning, the ski closest to the center of the turn is called the inside ski, the ski away from the center of the turn is called the outside ski. When turning on one ski, the weighted or turning ski is usually the outside ski. As the turn is begun, the outside ski is the uphill ski. But as the turn progresses and the skis cross the fall line, the outside ski becomes the downhill ski.

Weight on Both Feet

In the basic stance some weight is carried on each foot, although the amount of weight on each foot is constantly changing. The body maintains its balance by small shifts in weight from foot to foot. The weight distribution between the two feet at any one instant is usually not critical; the important point is that there should be some weight on each foot most of the time.

There are several reasons for weighting both feet:

1) *Better balance.* Just as better balance is achieved by distributing weight between the heel and ball of the foot, better balance is also maintained by standing on two feet instead of just one.

2) *Prevents drifting and crossing of the skis.* On packed slopes, moguls, and bumpy terrain, an unweighted uphill ski tends to drift, wander, and bounce. On steep slopes, an unweighted ski frequently does not turn at the same rate of speed as the weighted ski. When it turns too slowly, the tips of the skis cross; when it turns too quickly, the tails cross. By weighting both skis and rotating them together, these problems can be avoided *(Figure 30).*

3) *Stability in powder.* In deep powder, an unweighted ski will rise up out of the snow while the weighted ski lies deeper. Traveling with the two skis on different levels is uncomfortable and unstable.

4) *Each ski turns independently.* Modern skiing, and particularly racing, emphasizes that each ski can turn independently. In other words, although they turn simultaneously, each ski has its own turning forces. To achieve independent action, each ski must carry some weight.

Weighting the Downhill Ski and the Outside Ski

Many skiers were taught to keep most of their weight on the downhill ski (or the outside ski). Some were told to keep all of their weight on the outside ski. This emphasis on weighting the outside ski is a carryover from snowplow and stem turns. As mentioned in Chapter 4, to initiate a turn with a stem, place the turning ski (the stemmed ski) in the new direction and set that ski on its inside edge. Most or all of the body weight is then transferred to the stemmed ski to begin the turn. In the stem turn, only the stemmed ski does the turning. The other ski merely follows. To emphasize this point, many skiers were taught to lift the inside ski off the ground to make sure the outside ski did all the work.

In progressing from stem turns to parallel turns, many skiers have continued to retain the weighted outside ski and unweighted inside ski. Not only is this unnecessary but it makes parallel turning more difficult. In parallel turns, both feet turn simultaneously. There-

Figure 30

Weighting Uphill Ski

A) This skier has all his weight on the downhill ski. His unweighted uphill ski easily wanders. Because the downhill leg is so much lower than the uphill leg, it is difficult to flex the downhill knee. The straight downhill leg prevents good edging and causes undesirable sideslipping. **B)** This skier has weighted both his feet. The uphill ski no longer drifts. In addition, the increased flexion by the uphill leg permits this ski to be edged further into the hill than the downhill ski, and provides better edge control.

A. Uphill Ski Not Weighted

B. Uphill Ski Weighted

fore, you should not concentrate on keeping all weight on the outside ski. Instead, try to keep some weight on each foot.

Weighting the Uphill Ski and the Inside Ski

This chapter has stressed the importance of weighting both feet, although the distribution need not be equal. In stem turning, more weight must be carried on the outside ski. When traversing a slope, it is usually easier to carry more weight on the downhill ski. But when parallel turning, it is often advantageous to keep a fair amount of weight on the uphill ski. The steeper the slope, the more important it is to weight the uphill ski. On the steepest slopes, smoother and faster turns can sometimes be performed by placing most of the weight on the uphill ski. The reason for this is that the two legs are at different levels, resulting in the uphill leg having much more knee flexion than the downhill leg. On steep slopes, if most of the weight is carried on the downhill ski, edge control is difficult because of inadequate knee flexion. And it is hard to get more knee flexion from the downhill leg because the uphill knee cannot flex much further. On the other hand, the deeply flexed uphill knee is in excellent position to be pushed into the hill to set its outside edge. If the flexed uphill ski is also weighted, it can carve the turn more easily and quickly than the downhill ski *(Figure 30).*

In summary, the flexed leg is the one that can provide better edging. However, it can only provide better edging if it is weighted.

The same principle applies to banking high-speed turns: a flexed and weighted inside leg can give better edge control than a straight outside leg. Racers going through slalom gates sometimes weight their inside ski because the outside ski cannot edge as well as the inside ski *(Figure 31).*

A word of caution: The disadvantage of putting all weight on the uphill or inside ski is that you may lean too far uphill. This can result in undesirable sideslipping or falling. Avoid this by keeping a little weight on the other ski.

Weighting Both Feet in Carving

When carving a turn, the arc in the ski is determined by the weight on the ski. When the skis are equally weighted, both skis will have the same curve. If more weight is shifted to one ski, the arc in that ski will in-

Figure 31

Weighting Inside vs. Outside Ski

A) A racer banking a turn with all his weight on the outside ski. The inside leg and thigh must be advanced to keep them out of the way. The edgeset of the outside ski cannot be increased because the knee is almost straight. This may prevent the skier from executing a sharp turn without skidding. **B)** This racer is banking the same turn with most of his weight on the inside ski. Because this knee is more flexed than the outside knee, it is capable of more edgeset and a sharper carved turn. The outside ski lags a little behind and does not interfere with the turn.

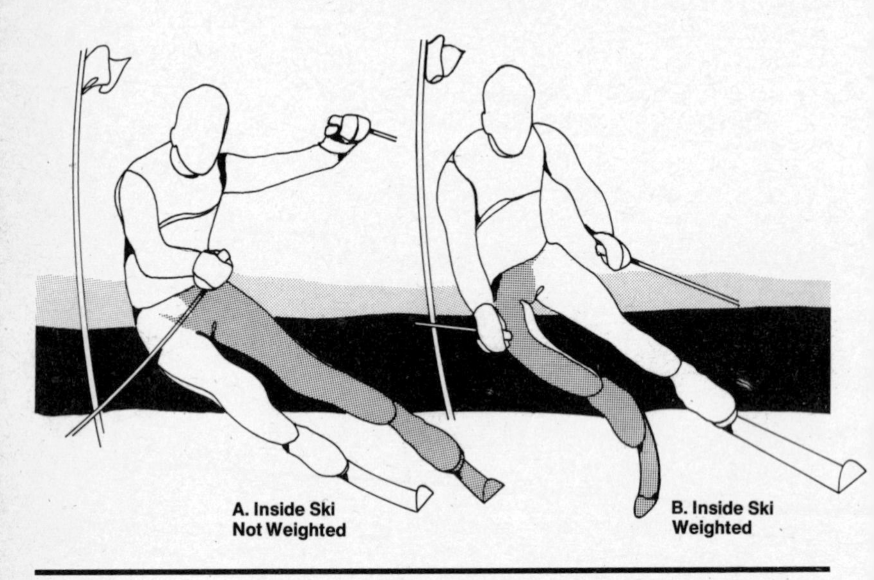

crease, and a sharper turn can be carved. In powder, it is best to ski with both feet equally weighted. But on packed slopes, there is a choice between equal weighting or predominantly weighting one ski. Accomplished skiers should be capable of skiing both ways and of selecting the technique that seems most effective for the slope and snow conditions.

Advancing the Uphill Ski

Advancing the uphill ski a few inches ahead of the downhill ski is a common practice. When your upper body is facing downhill with the skis pointing across the hill, the uphill hip leads the downhill hip. Therefore, the uphill ski will naturally tend to lie a couple of inches ahead. However, when your upper body faces the ski tips and is square to the hips, there is little reason to force the uphill ski ahead.

In general, advancing the uphill ski is a minor point. Use it where it feels comfortable.

Feet a Few Inches Apart

When skiing with all your weight on one ski, it may make sense to lock your knees and feet together. In this way, as the weighted ski turns, the unweighted ski accompanies it. However, when both feet are weighted, there is no value in keeping your feet touching. The main reason for keeping weight on each foot is better stability; if your feet are next to each other, some of this advantage is lost. By spreading your feet a few inches apart, a wider base is acquired which provides better balance.

In summary, skiing with some weight on both the uphill and downhill ski, and with your feet a few inches apart, will provide optimum stability and balance.

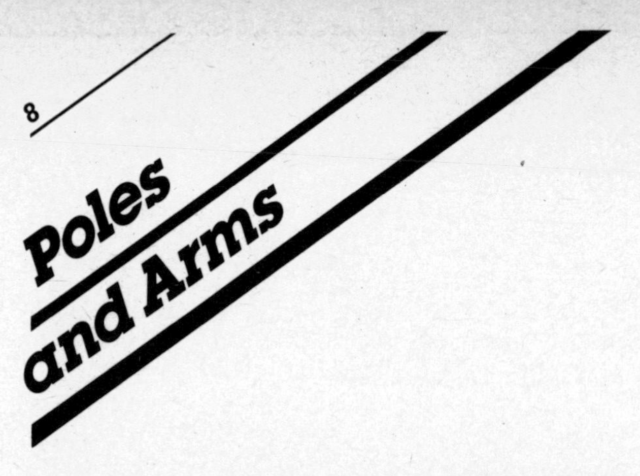

Summary: The arms and poles should be held in front of your body. Their main purpose is for balance during unweighting. Therefore, plant the pole just before unweighting.

It is possible to ski without using ski poles. Some skiers carry poles in their hands but don't use them. Beginners often find it simpler to learn to ski without poles. However, using ski poles makes turning easier, especially on steep, bumpy terrain. The proper use of ski poles is an essential element of good skiing.

The primary purpose of the ski pole is to maintain balance during the moment of unweighting. If you learned to ski without poles, you can add the poles when learning to unweight.

The pole plant is both a timing device and a stabilizer, giving the upper body a post to lean upon. When making quick, short turns, the pole plant is just a timing device. Place the pole in the snow just prior to unweighting and rapidly remove it. It does not remain in the snow long enough to support any of the body's weight. On the other hand, when you are making longer, more complete turns, and particularly at slower speeds, the stabilizing effects of the pole plant become more important. With the pole in the snow, you can place some of your weight on the pole by pressing hard against the snow with the poling arm. If your legs are unweighted at the same instant your arm is pushing down on the pole, it can support a portion of the body's weight. Your unweighted legs can then pivot and change their edges, while the upper body is stabilized by the pole plant.

Precisely where you plant the pole varies. When

Pole Plant Using Wrist

Figure 32

The wrist is cocked up to plant the pole ahead of the foot. The pole is released by skiing past the basket and bending the wrist downward. The shoulder does not fall behind the line of the back.

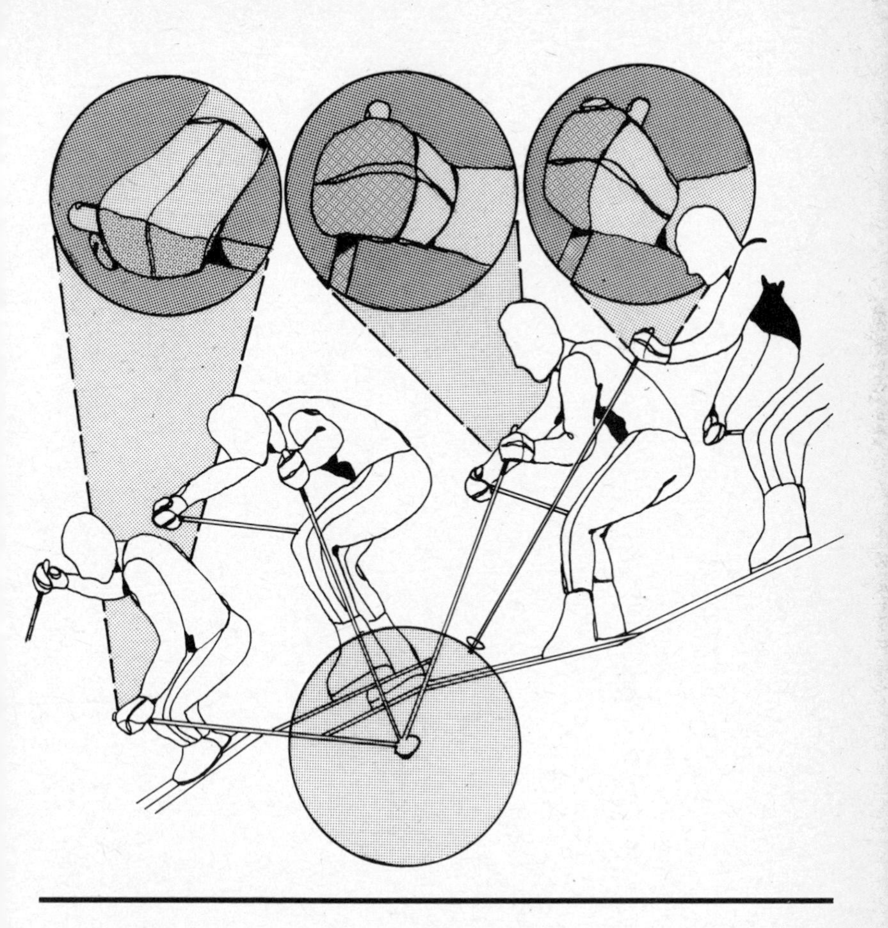

used for timing only, it can be planted at any comfortable spot next to or ahead of your feet. As a general rule, at fast speeds and for long-radius (wide-arc) turns, the downhill pole is planted a couple of feet ahead of the downhill boot. At slow speeds and for short-radius turns, the pole is planted closer to the boot. In planting the pole ahead, your shoulder should not move, as this will turn your shoulders uphill. Only your arm and elbow are extended. The pole is then placed forward by cocking your wrist upward.

Once you plant the pole, your feet will pass by the basket quickly, but you should not let your shoulder be rotated by the pole. Instead, your arm should be held in front of your body throughout the turn. As you move past the pole, your wrist should be bent downward, placing the pole at a constantly changing angle to the snow. The pole will eventually lift up by itself *(Figure 32).*

Timing the pole plant is important. The proper moment is just before unweighting. When UP-unweighting, the pole is planted just as the UP movement begins *(Figure 17).* When DOWN-unweighting, the pole is planted a split second before dropping the seat DOWN *(Figure 18).*

Summary: Banking, or inward lean toward the center of the turn, is another method of edge control. It can only be used when moving with some speed.

In addition to knee angulation and hip angulation (Chapter 1), edge setting can be achieved by leaning inward against centrifugal force. If one makes a left turn while skiing with some speed, the body will feel a force pulling it to the right. This force, which always pulls away from the center of the turn, is called centrifugal force. To counteract centrifugal force, the entire body can lean to the left in the direction of the turn. This will increase the degree of edging. The higher the speed, the larger the centrifugal force, and the greater the angle at which the body can lean to increase edge setting. At slow speeds there is less centrifugal force, so the body cannot lean as far, and therefore, less edging is possible.

Leaning in the direction of the turn is called *banking.* It is the same action used by a bicyclist or a skater when making a turn at fast speeds. The cyclist and the skater also lean their bodies toward the center of the turn to counteract centrifugal force *(Figure 33).*

Banking transfers weight to the edges of the skis. This results in edging, the same edging that is accomplished by knee angulation or hip angulation. Good skiers use all of these methods for edge control, sometimes separately, at other times together *(Figure 34).* Compared to knee angulation, banking uses less energy, requires more time, and must be corrected (by straightening up) when the turn is completed or when the skier slows down. Edge setting by knee angulation requires more work by the thigh muscles, but it provides faster edging, finer control, and easier adjust-

Figure 33

Banking

Banking is leaning inward, toward the center of the turn, to counteract centrifugal force. At higher speeds, greater degrees of banking are possible. A skier banks just like a cyclist does.

ment of the edges. Hip angulation is the least important means of edging and is seldom used alone. It should be regarded as a secondary method of edge control which can supplement the primary forms—knee angulation and banking.

Banking has limitations. It cannot be used at slow speeds because there is not enough centrifugal force to counteract. Further, banking is limited only to the time the skier is turning, as the inward lean must be corrected to an upright position when centrifugal force is dissipated. Hence, at slow speeds and when you are not turning, knee angulation must be used for edging.

Banking is commonly used to stop. Banking, in

Banking

Figure 34

Banking is performed by leaning the upper body inward, in the direction of the turn. In this picture, the skier is also angulating his knees and hips inward to increase the degree of edgeset. (Copper Mountain photo by Rick Godin.)

combination with knee and hip angulation, will produce maximum edging and the quickest stop. But as speed is reduced en route to stopping, the inward lean must be gently corrected to an upright position. Failure to straighten up soon enough results in falling uphill. This is a common cause for falling: too much uphill lean for too slow a speed.

Summary: The three rules of deep powder skiing are 1) turns must be completed by carving, not skidding; 2) there must never be more weight on the toes than on the heels; and 3) both feet should be equally weighted.

Skiing in deep powder is one of the real thrills in skiing. It is a unique sensation to ski through bottomless soft snow, a sensation that is seldom experienced on packed slopes. There is a feeling of absolute control because the texture of the powder is usually consistent. When setting your edges into deep snow you feel a smooth resistance which is the same throughout the turn. You know that in each turn you will encounter the same dependable resistance as the previous turn. You needn't worry about your edges slipping on a hard or icy spot, since there aren't any icy spots in deep powder. Your mind and body can relax as you glide smoothly along.

One often hears that "skiing powder is just like skiing on packed snow, except you sit further back." For some skiers this statement is true, but for others, it is not. The reason for this is that there is only one way to complete a turn in deep powder, while there are two ways on packed snow. In powder, the skier should follow the direction of the tips of the skis through a turn. This is called carving. On packed snow, the skier may complete turns either by carving or by skidding (following the sides of the skis). Appreciating the difference between skidding and carving is THE essence of learning powder skiing. Most skiers who ski on packed slopes turn by skidding with the sides of their skis leading the turn. Although this is effective on packed snow, it is often ineffective in deep powder because deep powder resists any lateral movements of the ski. Thus, the skier who carves turns on packed slopes can use the same technique in powder. But the skier who turns by skidding will have difficulty in powder and must learn the technique of carving.

The first part of this chapter on powder skiing deals with the principles of powder skiing, and the second describes how to apply them. An understanding of powder skiing begins with a look at the effects of packed and powder snow on the bottoms and the edges of the skis.

Firm Versus Soft Base

A packed slope has a firm, noncompressible base. Any ski that lies on this base will lie flat against the hard surface. A flexible ski will lie just as flat as a stiff ski. In deep powder, say over two feet, the ski rests on a much different base. The snow beneath the ski is soft and compressible, like a sponge. The skier's weight presses the ski into the snow until it is supported on a base of loosely packed snow. The stiff ski and the flexible ski will now conform in different ways to this soft base. The stiff ski distributes the skier's weight fairly evenly across the length of the ski so that the ski will sink evenly into the soft snow, continuing to lie almost flat against the soft base. In contrast, the weight is not evenly distributed on a flexible ski. It remains centered under the foot with less weight at the tip and tail of the ski. The middle of the ski will therefore drop deeper into the snow than the two ends, producing an arc *(Figure 35).*

A ski resting on powder is similar to a board resting on a mattress. If a person stands in the center of the board, the board will sink a few inches into the mattress. If the board is very stiff, it will sink fairly evenly into the mattress, maintaining its straight line. However, if the board is flexible, the center of the board, under the feet, will sink deeper than the ends of the board, producing an arc *(Figure 36).*

In powder, the arc in a flexible ski directs the ski tip upward, towards the surface of the snow. By using a flexible ski, you can keep your weight in the middle of your foot and still keep the ski tip from diving deeper under the snow. When using a stiff ski, it is often necessary to move your weight a little further back, to-

Figure 35

Stiff vs. Flexible Ski

Top) In deep snow, a stiff ski distributes the skier's weight fairly evenly throughout the ski. Only a minimal curve is formed in the ski. **Bottom)** The flexible ski keeps more of the skier's weight in the center of the ski. This produces a greater curve. When the skis are rolled onto their edges, this arc will be followed to carve turns in powder.

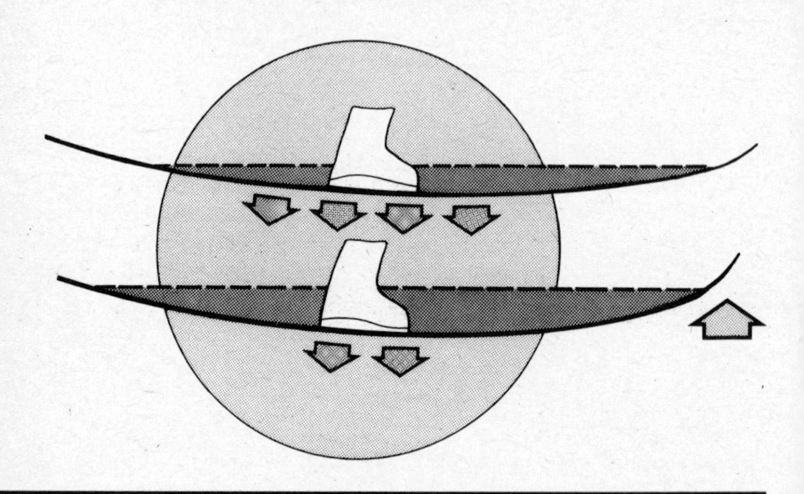

wards your heel, to prevent the tip from diving. Therefore, in deep powder, using a flexible ski makes it easier to maintain your balance.

Three Rules of Powder

Once you have seen how skis are affected by deep powder, the three rules of powder become clear. 1) Turns must be completed by carving because deep snow offers too much resistance to skidding. 2) There must never be more weight on the toes than on the heels or the ski tips will dive deep. 3) Both feet should be equally weighted to permit the skis to sink to the same depth in the snow. Otherwise one ski will lie deeper than the other.

Shallow Powder

Deep powder means there is still soft uncompressed snow below the compressed layer supporting the skis. Shallow powder implies that all of the soft snow beneath the skis is compressed against the base, so that a rather firm base supports the bottoms of the skis.

The firm base under the skis makes shallow powder different from deep powder in two ways. First, the tips of the skis cannot dive any deeper, as there is already

Stiff vs. Flexible Board

Figure 36

Top) The stiff board distributes weight evenly across the board, so no arc develops. **Bottom)** The flexible board carries most of the weight in the center, less at the ends. The resulting curve is a marked contrast from the stiff board.

a firm base under them. Therefore, if too much weight is transferred to the toes, falling forward will not occur in shallow powder the way it would in deep powder. Secondly, the firm base under shallow powder permits carving turns by the same mechanism that is used on packed slopes. The side-cut of the edged ski allows the tip and tail of the ski to grip the base. This permits the suspended center of the ski to be pushed downward by the skier's weight, producing an arc in the ski. Therefore, the stiff ski can develop more of an arc for carving turns in shallow powder than it can in deep powder. The flexible ski works well in both.

Although shallow powder differs in some respects from deep powder, there is one principle that remains the same in all types of powder—the need to carve. In shallow powder, just as in deep powder, sideways movement by skidding or sideslipping encounters more resistance than forward movement by carving. When the leading part of the ski is the side of the ski rather than the tip, the side is still breaking through soft powder, in spite of the firm base under the ski. The depth and weight of the soft snow become important factors in the amount of resistance meeting the side of the ski. A few inches of shallow and light powder will have little effect on skidding and sideslipping. But as the powder gets deeper and heavier, sideways movement becomes increasingly difficult, and following the ski tips through a carved turn is the easiest—and frequently the only—way.

Balance in Powder

Maintaining good balance is essential for deep-powder skiing. This is the most difficult aspect of powder skiing to master. You should carry your weight on both the heels and the balls of your feet. Keep your weight forward by flexing your ankles and pushing your shins against your boot tops. Then drop your seat by flexing your knees until you feel enough weight on your heels to keep the ski tips pointing slightly upward. In deep powder it is essential that the balls of the feet never have more weight than the heels. If they do, your ski tips will dive deeper, causing you to fall head first. But do not put *all* of your weight on your heels. This is unnecessary and makes it difficult to maintain balance. Powder skiing is more comfortable and more stable when some of your weight pushes against your boot tops, and a little more weight is felt on your heels. The correct balance between heels and toes is the distribution that will let the ski tips point slightly upward, towards the surface *(Figure 37, also Figures 5 and 6).*

Ski equipment is an important factor in maintaining balance in powder. In addition to a flexible ski, the location of your ski binding affects balance. In deep powder, the toe binding should lie about one cm behind the center of balance of the ski. If the binding is mounted too far forward, even one or two cm, your ski

Position in Powder

Figure 37

Knee flexion and ankle flexion combine to keep the weight balanced across the feet. In the proper stance you should feel the pressure of your shins against your boot tops and also some weight on your heels. How much weight? Just enough to keep your ski tips pointing towards the surface of the snow.

tips will tend to dive deep when your weight is in the center of the ski. It then becomes necessary to transfer more weight to your heels, a position which is unstable and difficult to hold.

In shallow powder, the requirements for good balance are a little different. Your weight may be evenly distributed, as it is not essential that the ski tips point upwards. Even if the tips carry a little more weight than the heels, the firm base under the shallow powder will prevent the tips from diving deeper into the snow. However, beware of shallow powder that suddenly gets deeper. If your weight is forward, you will fall. Therefore, it is best to ski all types of powder with your weight evenly distributed or with a *little* more weight on your heels.

Turning in Powder

Initiating Turns

Turns in powder, as on packed snow, can be initiated by rotating the feet or by changing edges (see Chapter 4). Rotating the feet (foot twist) is more difficult in powder snow because of the resistance of the snow to the sideways movement of the edge of the ski. For this reason, hip rotation, hip projection, and even shoulder rotation must at times be added to twist the skis in powder. During rotation the skis should be flat, not edged.

Changing edges is the easiest way to initiate a turn in powder. There is much less resistance to rolling the edges from side to side than to pivoting the skis. Edge change followed by carving is the smoothest path through deep powder. However, these turns have a long radius. When tighter turns are needed, a quick rotation to initiate the turn should be used.

Unweighting in powder is no different from on packed snow. Up-unweighting, down-unweighting, or leg retraction can be used as desired. However, when initiating sharp turns in heavy powder, a long, forceful foot, hip, and sometimes shoulder rotation is needed. When this is the case, up-unweighting will provide the longest time interval for rotation. When the powder is soft, down-unweighting or leg retraction will give you a quicker turn and better control.

Completing Turns

Carving is done by turning your skis onto their edges, primarily by rolling your flexed knees to the side (knee angulation, *Figure 38*). At fast speeds, carving can also be done by leaning your body inward towards the center of the turn or banking *(Figure 33)*.

In deep or shallow powder, the degree of edging determines the length of the turn. The further you angulate your knees to the side, the greater the "edgeset," the more the arc in your skis, and the sharper the turn. In very shallow, light powder, say one to six inches, skidded turns may work well because the skis are resting

Knee Angulation to Complete Turns in Powder

Figure 38

To complete turns in powder, roll your knees to the side, keeping both feet equally weighted.

on a hard base and there is not much resistance to sideways motion. However, carved turns will also work well.

Turns on Steep Slopes

On steep hills, the pull of gravity is often strong enough to overcome the resistance of the deep snow to lateral movement of the skis. On steep slopes some skidding usually occurs, particularly when making wide-angle turns. However, skidding in powder happens naturally, with the skis sideslipping downhill in a continuation of the initial turning force. In deep powder, you cannot use leverage; you cannot momentarily transfer your weight forward to your ski tips to let the tails pivot around the tips because your tips will dive and you will fall over, head first. When skidding in powder, you must keep your weight in the middle of the skis and prepare yourself to stop the skid by quickly rolling your knees into the hill. This checking in powder will provide a platform from which you can unweight and pivot your feet when you start the next turn.

In deep powder on very steep slopes you can initiate turns by either edge change or rotation. However, edge change will start a gradual turn, often too gradual to prevent acceleration. The only way you can then reduce speed is to rotate your hips and shoulders in the middle of the turn to face your skis across the hill. This produces a skid which slows you down, but also leaves your shoulders pointing uphill, unprepared for the next turn.

The preferred technique for turning on steep slopes is to initiate your turn with rotation preceded by anticipation. This produces a sharper turn, it prevents acceleration, and it lets you complete the turn by rolling your edges into the hill. This will carve the end of the turn. Your skis may skid automatically as you complete the turn, but your action should be to simply roll your knees into the hill, keep your upper body facing downhill, and prepare to check and initiate your next turn.

Learn Powder Skiing on Packed Slopes

All the techniques for skiing in powder can be practiced on packed slopes. Concentrate on standing on both feet with your weight equally distributed between the heels and the balls of your feet. As you turn, do not shift your weight from foot to foot, and do not lean forward. Try to keep your weight centered and balanced all the time. Carve as much of the completion of your turns as possible. Think about angulating your knees into the hill to set your edges and minimize sideslipping. If you can do it on packed snow, you can do it in powder.

Part II

Putting It All Together

11

Weight on the Outside Ski and Forward Lean

"Weight the outside ski" and "lean forward"—these are two of the most common "rules" in skiing. But these are two rules which should frequently be broken. They are useful in many situations but not all the time. This book puts very little emphasis on weighting the downhill ski and leaning forward. This approach is based on skiing in deep powder where both feet should be equally weighted and leaning forward can be catastrophic. If it is possible to ski in deep powder with smoothness and complete control without weighting the outside ski or leaning forward, why shouldn't it be possible on packed snow? The answer: it is.

It is true that on packed slopes weighting the outside ski and using forward leverage will make many turns easier. But it is also possible to perform these turns with your weight centered on both feet. Thus, weighting the outside ski and forward lean should be regarded as points of lesser importance, secondary to the more basic fundamentals of knee flexion, knee angulation, and good balance. They can be added as improvements or refinements in technique. Use these techniques judiciously. Weighting the outside ski means putting *more* weight on that foot but not all of your weight. Leaning forward means putting a *little more* weight on the balls of your feet, but never completely unweighting your heels.

Aside from falling, you can stop either by turning your skis across the hill or by snowplowing. The basic elements of parallel and stem turns are described in Chapters 13 and 15. Either of these can be used for stopping by completing the turn with a sideslip and an edgeset *(Figure 39)*.

Steering to a Stop

For the beginner, an easy way to turn and stop is to steer the skis until they lie across the hill, and stop them by sideslipping. Steering is performed by flexing your knees and pushing them sideways, in the direction of the turn (knee angulation). This sets the skis on their edges and begins turning them. Steering is also assisted by adding a twisting motion of the feet (see page 38, Steering). As the skis turn to lie perpendicular to the fall line, a sideslip is begun. The skis are then stopped by increasing knee angulation into the hill to check the sideslip *(Figure 40)*.

Snowplow

The snowplow or wedge is primarily a method for slowing and stopping. It is used by all skiers, as it is particularly needed on narrow trails and in tow lines. Because it is relatively easy to perform, the snowplow is often taught to beginners.

The features of the snowplow are: 1) knees and ankles flexed, 2) tips together, 3) tails apart, and 4) both skis set on their inside edges by rolling the knees toward each other. Once in the snowplow position, stopping and starting is controlled by the knees. To stop, the knees roll toward each other to increase the degree of edgeset. To start, the knees move apart, flattening the skis against the slope *(Figure 41)*.

A second motion can assist in stopping: forward

Parallel (Hockey) Stop

Figure 39

A basic parallel turn is begun with 1) up-unweighting, 2) foot twist, and 3) edging the skis until they sideslip to a stop.

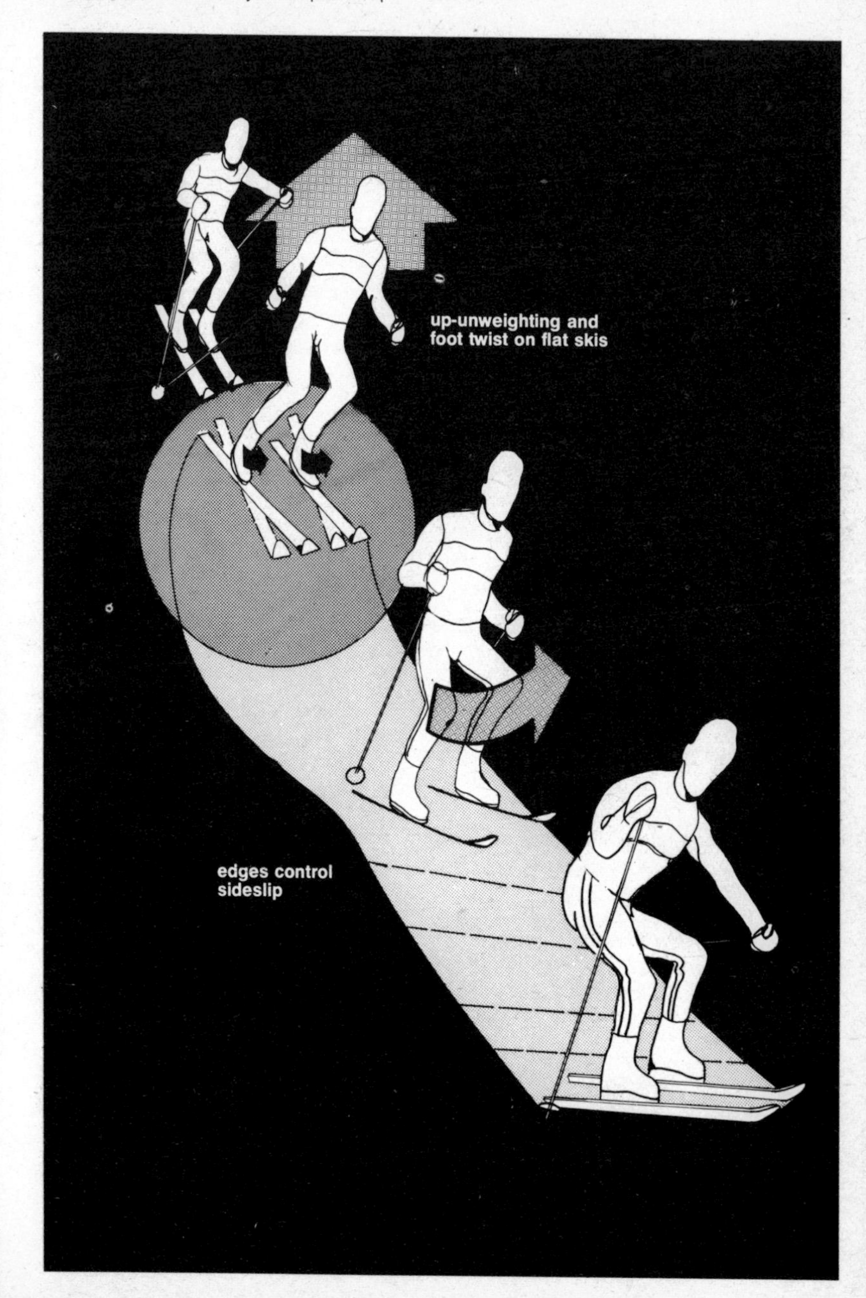

Figure 40

Steering to a Stop

With the skis heading downhill, the knees are both flexed and angulated to one side. In addition, an attempt is made to twist the feet and legs in the direction of the turn. As the skis change direction, a sideslip and check is needed to stop. This is done by increasing knee angulation and edgeset.

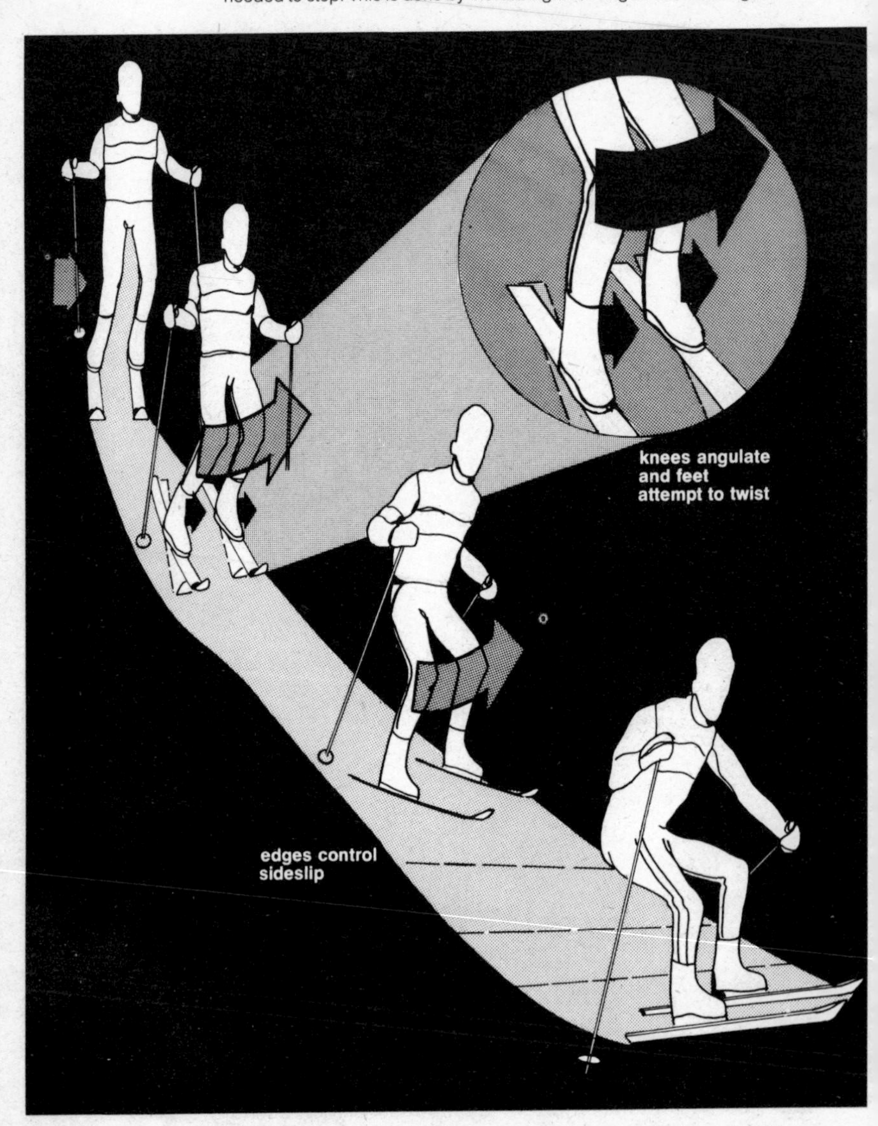

lean (forward leverage). By increasing ankle flexion and pushing your shins against your boot tops, weight is transferred forward to the balls of your feet, un-

Snowplow Stop

Figure 41

To glide downhill, the knees are separated to flatten the skis on the snow. To slow down and stop, turn the skis onto their inside edges by pushing the knees toward each other as well as pushing the knees forward. Feel your shins press against your boot tops.

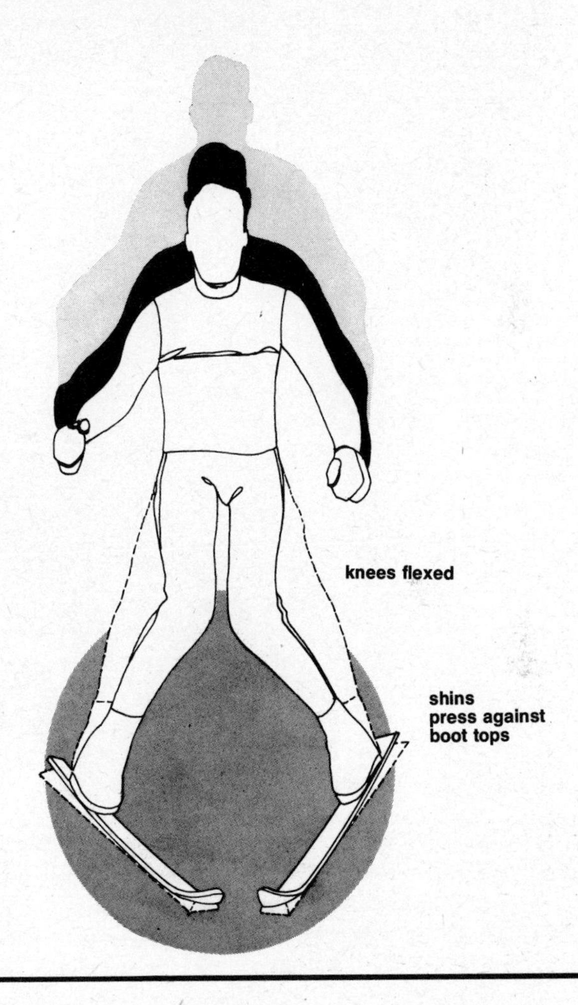

weighting the heels. This increased weight on the tips makes them grasp the slope, while the tails tend to separate. The further the tails spread apart, the closer the skis come to lying perpendicular to the fall line. This increases the pressure of the edges against the slope, assisting stopping. To increase speed, weight is transferred back to the center of your feet.

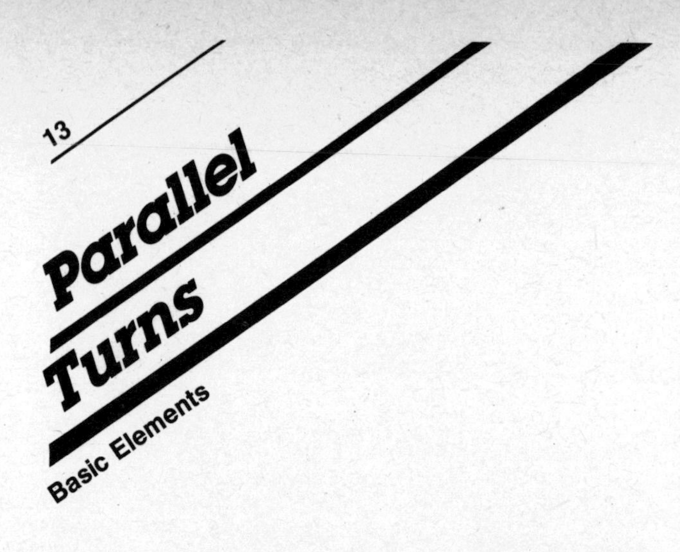

The beginner can learn to ski by starting with either parallel or stem turns, although both techniques should eventually be learned. In the past, the stem turn was regarded as an essential first step in learning parallel turns. However, as Clif Taylor has shown in his book *GLM—The New Way to Ski* (New York: Grosset & Dunlap, 1973), this is not necessary. Parallel turns can be learned first.

In a parallel turn, both feet change direction simultaneously. In its simplest form, the parallel turn has three elements which are performed in sequence: 1) unweighting, by a quick hop up; 2) foot rotation, by twisting both feet in the direction of the turn; and 3) edging, by flexing the knees and angulating them uphill. Proper balance is necessary; the weight should be centered on each foot and distributed between the two feet. Each of these points will be discussed below.

Balance

A correct ski position starts with knees and ankles flexed, and the waist bent forward. Your goal is to keep your weight centered on your feet. Dropping your seat, by flexing your knees, puts more weight on your heels. Pushing your knees forward, by flexing your ankles, places more weight on the balls of your feet. You can combine knee flexion and ankle flexion by simply *dropping your seat over your heels.* This will distribute your weight fairly evenly between the heels and balls of your feet. You should feel two things: Your shins

Correct Body Stances

Figure 42

All of the positions shown here are proper stances. They each fulfill the criteria of having some knee flexion and maintaining equal weight distribution between the heels and balls of the feet. In A and B, each degree of knee flexion is balanced by a corresponding degree of ankle flexion. In C, with 90° of knee flexion, waist flexion must be added to ankle flexion to maintain proper balance because ankle flexion cannot transfer as much weight forward as knee flexion transfers backward (Chapter 2).

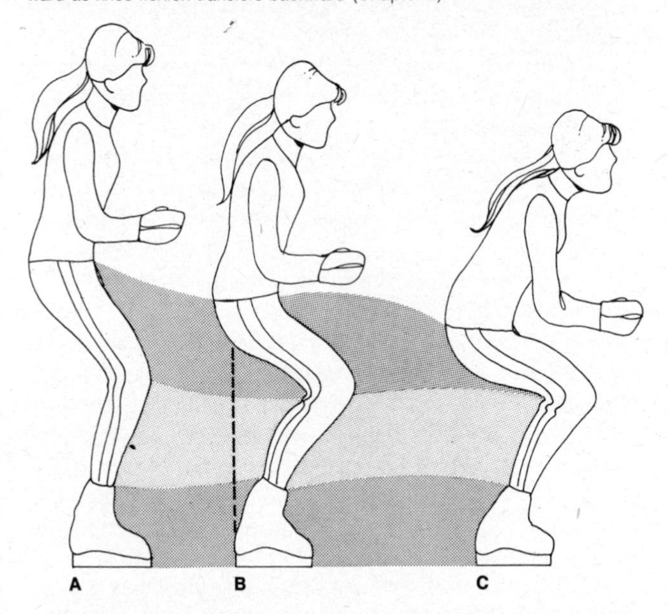

pushing against your boot tops and some pressure on your heels. Adjust these two until they are about equal.

Several body positions are correct *(Figure 42)*, and a good skier will use most of them on any given day. On steep slopes or when turning sharply, try to use more knee and ankle flexion. When your leg muscles are tired or you are skiing on gentle slopes, it is less strenuous to ski in a more erect position. But although your body position is constantly changing, the basic principle of balance between the heels and balls of your feet remains the same.

Good balance is achieved not only by correct weight distribution between the front and back parts of each foot, but also by proper distribution of weight between the two feet. In parallel turns, your weight should be on both feet, although the weight distribution need not be equal (see Chapter 7).

Unweighting

Hopping up or up-unweighting is the easiest way to learn to unweight. At a later stage, you can learn down-unweighting. Up-unweighting is a down-UP motion. First, drop your seat over your heels to increase knee flexion. Then *quickly* lift your seat back to its previous position without straightening your knees completely *(Figure 43).*

In learning to up-unweight, exaggerate the UP motion so that you can really FEEL the sensation of weightlessness. Once you feel what it is like to have a moment with no weight on your feet, practice a less vigorous UP motion, leaving your feet on the ground.

Rotation

Although you can rotate your body with your feet, knees, hips, or shoulders, you should learn foot rotation first. This is also called foot twist, swivel, or pivot. Both feet twist simultaneously in the direction of the turn. Foot rotation cannot be done easily when the feet are carrying the body's weight. Therefore, foot rotation should be performed when the feet are unweighted, with the "hop up" action just described.

Shoulder rotation may be added to foot rotation to assist the turn. However, you should not regard shoulder rotation *with the turn* as an important turning force. As your ability improves, you will learn to initiate turns by rotating your lower body only, without rotating your shoulders. However, in difficult snow conditions, maximum rotation is occasionally needed and the shoulders can be used for "survival." In Chapter 16, the use of shoulder rotation *before the turn* (anticipation) will be discussed.

Edging—Knee Angulation

After the feet have unweighted and rotated, controlling the edges of the skis will complete the turn. Edge control requires two actions of the knees: 1) knee flexion and 2) knee angulation (see Chapter 1). With the knees flexed, the edges of the skis can complete the turn by either skidding or carving, as discussed in Chapter 17.

Practice Indoors—Use a Mirror

The basic skills—balance, unweighting, rotation and edging—can be practiced indoors. Try this in front of a mirror. For balance, drop your seat over your heels and notice how your knees and ankles must flex. Feel your shins push against the tongues of the boots and

Three Basic Elements of Parallel Turns

Figure 43

1) The turn begins with a down-UP motion to up-unweight. **2)** During unweighting, the feet rotate in the direction of the turn. **3)** Knee angulation completes the turn by controlling the edges of the skis as they either skid or carve.

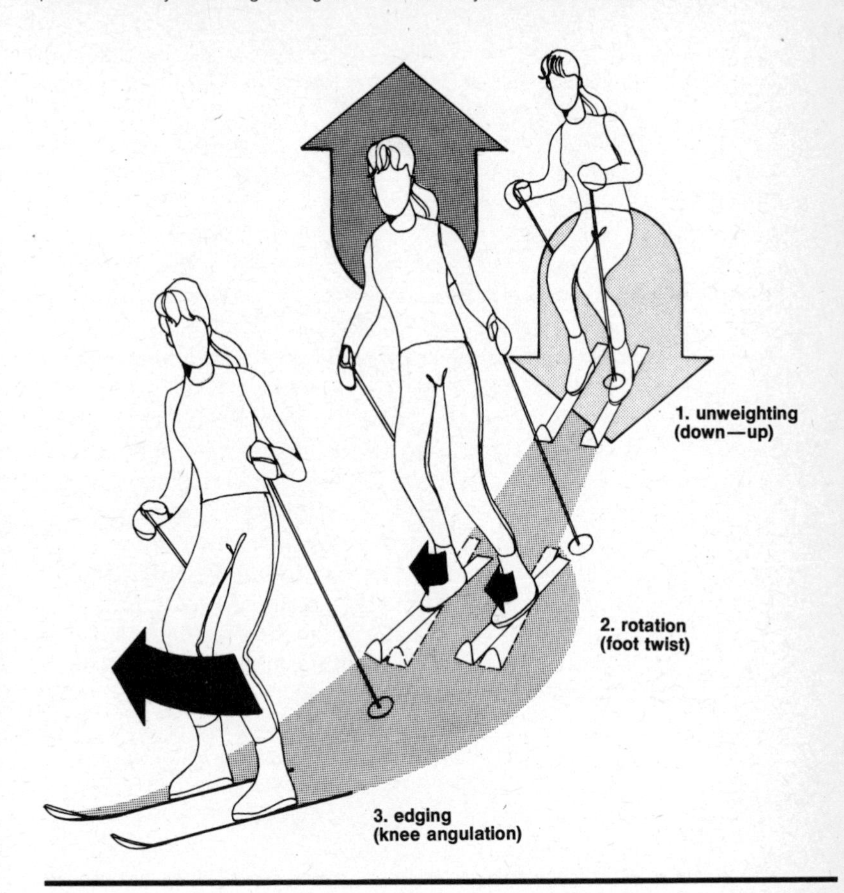

feel the pressure on your heels. Observe knee angulation by flexing your knees and rolling them to the side. Notice that the more you *flex* your knees, the further you can *angulate* them.

For UP-unweighting, practice the down-UP rhythm until you feel your feet unweight with less than four inches of vertical movement by your seat. Be sure that your knees never straighten. Foot rotation can be felt by sitting in a chair *(Figure 26)*.

14 Sidestepping and Sideslipping

Sidestepping

The parallel movement described in Chapter 13 is the first half of a turn. It changes the direction of the skis and resets their edges on the opposite side. The edges then complete the turn by skidding or carving (see Chapter 4). Each of these movements depends upon your ability to set and control your edges. One of the best and safest ways to learn the feeling of edging is by sidestepping.

Sidestepping is walking up or down a hill with the skis pointing across the hill. To maintain a position on a hillside without slipping, you must dig the uphill edges into the hill by *flexing the knees and moving them toward the slope (knee angulation).*

- *Stepping uphill.* Lift your uphill ski off the ground and step up the hill, setting the outside edge against the slope. Lean uphill with your hips, and momentarily put all your weight on the uphill ski. Quickly, bring your downhill ski up to the uphill ski, setting the inside edge of the downhill ski against the slope. You then transfer all of your weight back to the downhill ski. Remember, this is much easier to perform if your knees are bent *(Figure 44).*
- *Stepping downhill.* Place all your weight on the outside edge of the uphill ski while your lower ski moves down the hill. The knee of your downhill ski remains slightly bent and angulates into the slope. Your weight is shifted downhill and supported by the inside edge of your downhill ski, which should be in position to dig into the slope. Your uphill ski, which is now unweight-

Sidestepping

Figure 44

In sidestepping, transferring weight from one ski to the other is done by hip movement. The edges of the skis are set into the hill by rolling the knees uphill to prevent the skis from sliding back down.

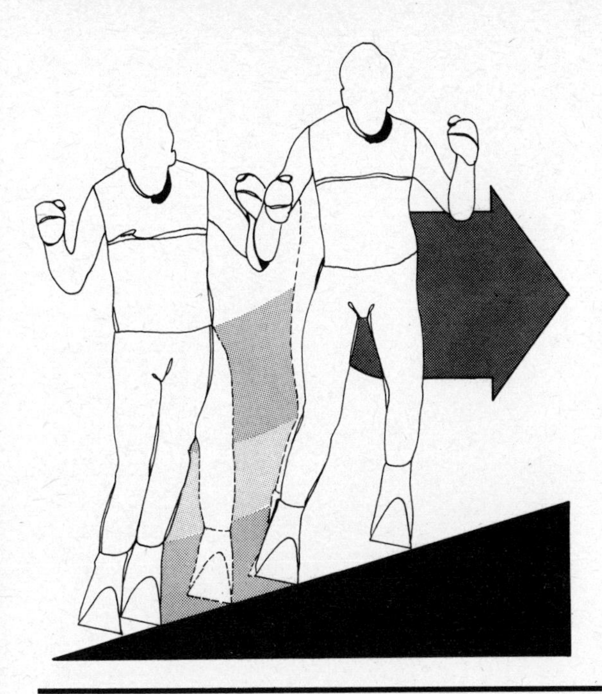

ed, can easily slide down to the downhill ski.

Additional points:

1) Use your poles for balance.

2) Keep your skis perpendicular to the fall line.

Sideslipping

Sideslipping, used to stop and slow down, involves sliding down a hill with the skis pointing across the hill. The fundamental action in sideslipping is controlling the skis' edges by rolling your knees uphill and downhill.

The traverse position is used in sideslipping. Begin by dropping your seat over your heels to keep your weight evenly distributed. Maintain some weight on each foot, but more on the downhill foot.

Knee angulation is the basic movement used in sideslipping. From the traverse position, push your knees downhill to partially flatten the skis against the slope

Figure 45

Sideslipping

In sideslipping, rolling the knees uphill to stop and downhill to slip is the key movement. The other parts of the body remain as quiet as possible. To begin slipping, the degree of edging is decreased. On gentle slopes, the skis may lie flat against the snow, but on steep slopes, the skis sideslip while still on their edges.

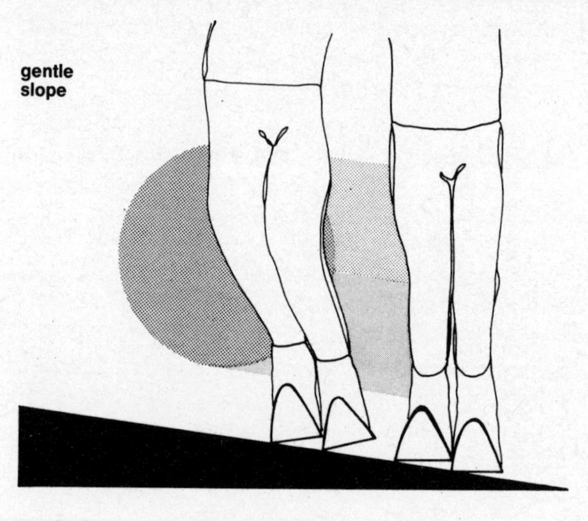

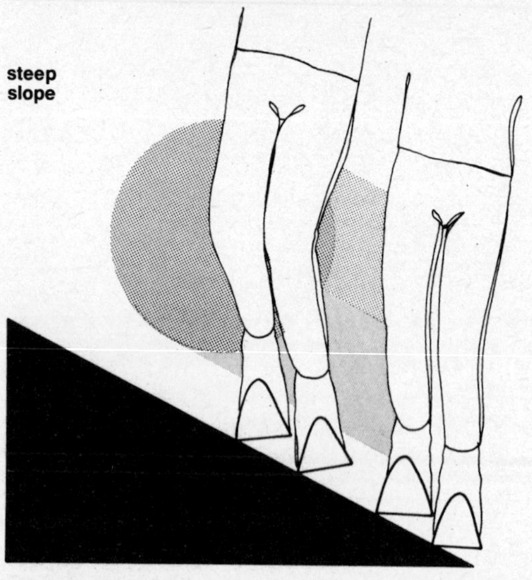

and permit sliding downhill. Stop the slide by angulating your knees back uphill to reset your edges into the slope. *Only your knees should move.* Your trunk and shoulders should remain centered over your skis *(Figure 45).* A small amount of hip movement often accompanies the knee movement, but this should be minimized.

Problems:

1) Getting started is often difficult. A steeper slope is best for practicing sideslipping. When standing sideways on gentle slopes, the pull of gravity is not strong enough to overcome the friction between skis and snow.

2) The uphill ski may not slide as easily as the downhill ski. This may be because the uphill ski has flattened too far and is catching its inside edge.

3) Flat ski or edged ski? The steepness of the slope determines how much or how little edgeset is needed to sideslip. On steep slopes it is anatomically impossible to flatten the skis against the hill. And considerable edging is needed to control the speed of the sideslip. On the other hand, sideslipping on gentle slopes requires minimal edgeset. The ski must lie almost flat against the hill to permit it to move at all. Thus, an edged ski is needed on steep slopes and a flat ski on gentle ones.

15 Stem and Snowplow Turns

Stem and snowplow turns should be learned by all skiers. Both use the same principles. The difference between them is that the snowplow turn is performed with both skis in the stem position, while in the stem turn, only the turning ski is stemmed. The snowplow turn is an excellent way to practice and feel edge control at slow speeds *(Figure 46).*

Stem turns should not be abandoned in spite of today's emphasis on learning to "ski parallel." In certain snow conditions parallel turns can be impossible and stemming must be used. Racers will often initiate a carved turn by stemming because it is faster and it keeps one ski in contact with the snow all the time.

A stem turn is initiated by one ski. The tail of that ski is pushed outward, the ski is placed on its inside edge facing in the new direction, and then the body's weight is transferred to the stemmed ski. There need not be a moment of unweighting, as in a parallel turn *(Figure 9).*

Stemming is done on the inside edge of either ski. Stemming the downhill ski turns you uphill and checks your speed. Stemming the uphill ski turns you downhill.

Downhill Stem (Abstem)

Stemming the downhill ski is a braking maneuver. It can also be used to prepare for the next turn. Beginning from a traverse, slide your downhill ski into a stem position. This is done by pressing your shin against your boot top so that your ski tip is weighted more than the tail. The tail can slip downhill while the tip bites the

Snowplow Turn

Figure 46

From a gliding snowplow position with the skis flat, flex your turning knee and push your leg forward against the boot top. Then roll the turning knee inward and drop your shoulder over the edged ski. As the outside ski begins carving a turn, keep the inside ski flat and minimally weighted.

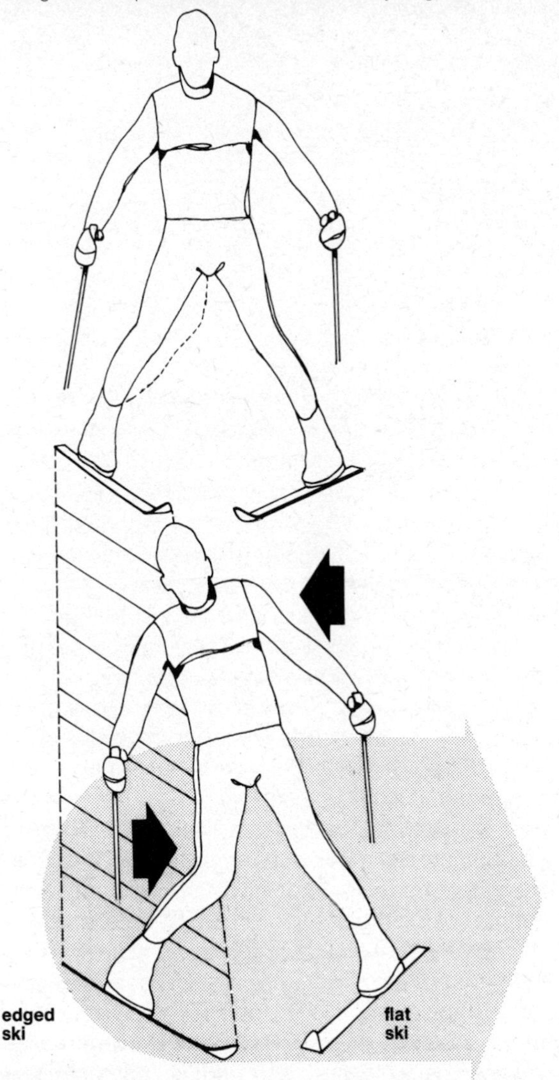

snow. It is easier to slide the ski out if it is flat, but it can also be stemmed when edged. Once in the stem position, edge the ski by rolling your downhill knee inward (knee angulation). Depending on the degree of edgeset, your ski can sideslip or be checked. The use of the downhill knee to control slippage is the same as discussed in the last chapter. Again, keeping the downhill knee flexed is a prerequisite for knee angulation.

Uphill Stem

Stemming the uphill ski will produce a turn without unweighting. Starting from a traverse position with flexed knees, the steps in performing a stem turn are as follows:

1) To begin the stem turn, put all of your weight on your downhill ski.

2) Stem the uphill ski by pushing the tail of the ski outward while the tip remains in place. Angulate the uphill knee inward to position the ski on its inside edge.

3) Transfer your weight from the downhill to the uphill ski. Your uphill ski (also called the outside ski) carries most of your weight as the turn begins *(Figure 9).*

4) The stem turn is completed by either skidding or carving as discussed in Chapters 4 and 17.

Stem to Parallel

The stem can be used as a stepping stone to a parallel turn. This is done by adding the element of unweighting to the downhill and uphill stem. Learn this turn on a gentle, flat slope. Start in a traverse position, but travel fast enough to permit your skis to glide easily when sideslipping. Therefore, your traverse should be partially directed downhill.

1) Stem the downhill ski and let it sideslip. This will reduce your speed. If you were already moving slowly, omit the sideslip.

2) Check the sideslip and perform a preparatory down motion. Do this by both dropping your seat over your heels and angulating your downhill knee into the hill. The seat drop is your down motion for down-UP unweighting. Knee angulation will set the inside edge of your ski to slow down your skid. As the ski stops (checks), you are ready to spring up. This position is called a platform and will be discussed again in Chapter 19.

3) Stem the uphill ski without weighting it. This can be done simultaneously with the down and check motions of the downhill stem. This prepares the uphill ski for the weight transfer.

4) Lift UP as you feel the edgeset of the downhill ski. This is up-unweighting and is performed by partially straightening the downhill knee.

5) Shift your weight to the uphill ski by shifting your hip uphill.

6) Complete the turn by skidding or carving, and slide the inside ski alongside the turning ski. Your turn will lead into a traverse where you can repeat the process.

Ski poles can be introduced with this turn if desired. They will assist unweighting. Plant the downhill pole about a foot ahead of the downhill foot. Plant it precisely at the moment of your edgeset, just as you start to lift up. The use of the pole is discussed more fully in the next chapter.

The stem turn with up-unweighting is still a stem turn. It is a one-legged turn with a weight shift from one leg to the other. The up-unweighting is not needed for the turn, but it's a gentle way to teach the feeling of up-unweighting.

The addition of unweighting to the stem turn does not produce a parallel turn. The key feature of a parallel turn is changing the direction of both skis *simultaneously*. The unweighting is done by both feet in unison. The initial turning action is often a twist of both feet, performed with both skis lying flat against the snow. Parallel turns are two-legged turns. In contrast, the stem turn does not offer these features. It is performed primarily by one ski lying on its edge, seldom flat. Foot twist is not a part of the stem turn.

The skier who can perform a good stem turn with up-unweighting has reached a plateau. To improve beyond this level it is necessary to look at a different concept in turning: "togetherness." Togetherness means unweighting, foot twisting, and edging both skis simultaneously. These basics are discussed in Chapters 13 and 16.

The basic elements in a parallel turn were outlined in Chapter 13. To improve your parallel turns, the same fundamentals must be restudied, but with greater emphasis on the details and proper timing of each action.

Initiating the Turn

Rotation

In general, the turning force in a parallel turn comes from rotation. It is true that you can also parallel turn by simply changing edges from one side to the other. However, this technique is limited to wide turns. (See Chapter 17.) The term "rotation" carries different meanings to different skiers. For many years rotation implied shoulder rotation. When ski schools began to emphasize rotation of the feet and eliminate rotation of the shoulders as the main turning force, the terms "foot twist," "foot swivel," and "foot pivot" developed. This new phraseology may have been designed to avoid the word rotation, which had become synonymous with shoulder rotation.

Rotation in parallel turns is used in two ways: 1) Prior to turning and prior to unweighting, rotating the shoulders to face downhill will greatly facilitate the beginning of a parallel turn. This early turning of the shoulders is called anticipation because the upper body anticipates the direction of the next turn. 2) During unweighting, when the body's weight is off the ground, rotation of the feet and legs will change the direction of the skis (foot twist).

Anticipation differs from conventional shoulder rotation because it precedes the turn. Anticipation is the first action in preparing to turn. It must precede unweighting because its effect is based on stretching the abdominal and back muscles. The tight muscles then turn the lower half of the body into the fall line during unweighting (see Chapter 6, *Figure 27*). Although anticipation is not essential, it makes turning faster and easier.

Anticipation

Foot twist is a main turning force and an essential action. However, it is very difficult to twist your skis with your full weight on them. Therefore, foot twist must be preceded by unweighting. At that instant, the feet can easily twist in the new direction. Emphasis here is on *timing*. If your feet have trouble pivoting, it is often because you did not unweight. Or, if you did unweight, you did so at the wrong time. Unweighting has but one purpose: to let your skis change direction with ease. You must twist your feet or change your edges *during* the moment of unweighting, or the unweighting action is wasted.

Foot Twist

Up-unweighting is probably the easiest type of unweighting for most people. An accomplished skier will use up-unweighting in some situations and down-unweighting in others. You will eventually want to learn both forms of unweighting, but it is easier to start with up-unweighting. Up-unweighting, in simplest terms, is taking the weight off your feet by hopping up. But it is a special kind of hop. It is a hop that lifts your seat without straightening your knees. The hop must be strong enough to lift the weight off your feet. To accomplish this, the hop must be quick. The emphasis in the movement is on *speed*—speed in the UP motion. It is possible to go through the down-UP maneuvers shown in Figure 17 without unweighting at all, if the UP movement is too slow. Thus, you can go through the motions without feeling the action.

Unweighting and Pole Plant

The ski poles are a helpful aid in unweighting and timing. If you haven't used your poles yet, this is a good time to start. Keep both elbows in front of your body. When turning left, plant your left pole a comfortable distance ahead of your left foot. The time of plant-

Figure 47

Simple Parallel Turn

From a traverse position, anticipate by facing your shoulders downhill. The down motion is followed by a pole plant which signals a quick lift up. While the feet are unweighted, they are twisted in the direction of the turn. In this example, the turn is being completed by carving.

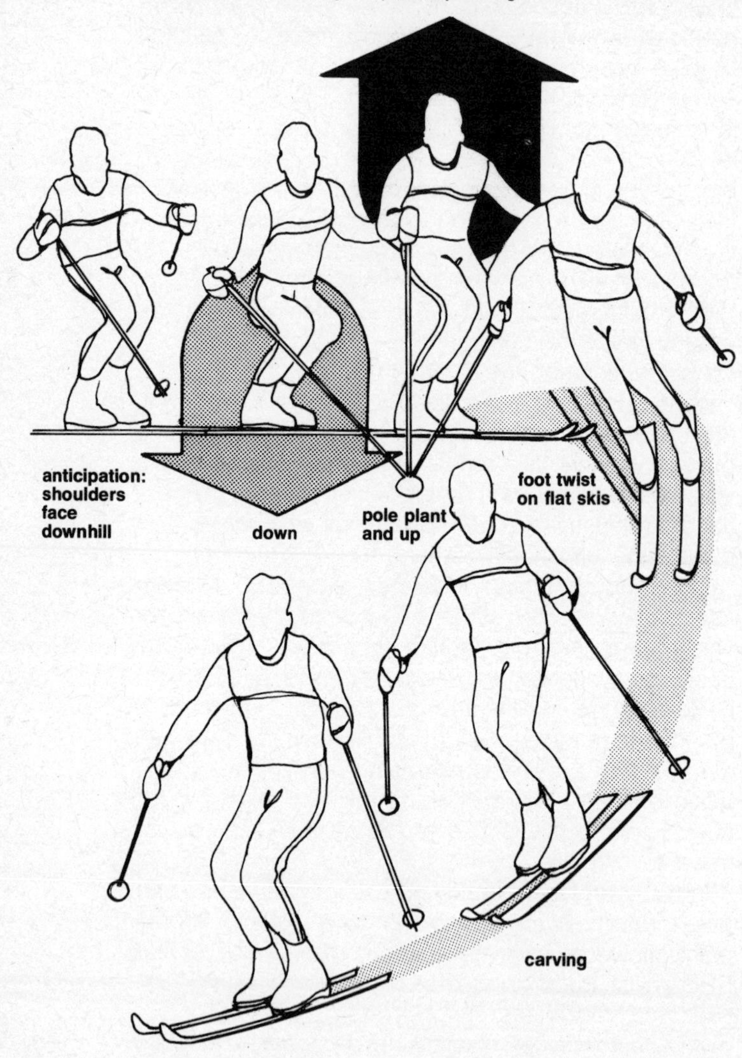

ing is important. Plant the pole just before lifting UP in your down-UP action.

The position of the pole plant varies with the speed and the radius of the turn. At slow speeds or for short-radius turns, plant the pole near the boot. At high speeds or for long-radius turns, plant it one to two feet ahead of the boot.

As discussed in Chapter 5, up-unweighting consists of two movements (down-UP). Starting with your knees bent, first lower your seat another three or four inches, keeping your weight centered. This is a preparatory action. Second, lift UP quickly. The seat is raised and the knees partially straightened but only to their original position. The knees should not straighten completely. The first movement—"down"—can be slow or fast. Its only purpose is to increase knee flexion. Knee flexion then permits the second movement—"UP"—to be performed without straightening the knees. The "UP" motion must be fast because this is where the unweighting occurs.

Anticipation and the down motion may be slow. But once the pole is planted, the UP motion and foot twist must follow in rapid succession. Once the pole is planted, the length of time it can remain in the snow is very limited, as you will rapidly ski past the basket and have to release the pole. Thus, at the instant the pole is planted the turn should begin.

In addition to timing, the pole plant assists the turn in two ways: as you lift UP, a portion of your weight can lean on the pole, thereby helping you unweight. Secondly, while you are unweighted, the planted pole helps balance and stabilize your body. Unweighting's purpose is to get the weight off your feet so they can twist. Putting some weight on your pole should not interfere with this. However, if you have too much weight on the pole, you will lose your balance when you remove it.

In summary, there are five steps in the first half of a parallel turn: 1) anticipation 2) down-motion 3) pole plant followed immediately by 4) a *quick* UP-motion and 5) foot twist. Performing these in sequence is essential. Make sure your knees remain flexed *(Figure 47).*

Completing the Turn

Weight on Both Feet

After you have unweighted and twisted your feet, the weight will return to your feet. It is important to return weight to *both* feet. Many people were taught to ski with all of their weight on the downhill ski. This is a carry-over from the one-legged stem turn and does not apply to the two-legged parallel turn (see Chapter 7). There is no reason to routinely shift weight from one foot to the other in a parallel turn. In many situations you will have more weight on one foot than the other. But you should try to keep some weight on each foot. If you have been skiing with all of your weight on one ski, this is a good time to change that habit.

Pole Release and Facing Downhill

Once you've skied past the pole's basket, the pole ceases to be a help and can be released. This is best done by keeping your elbow and arm in front of your body and simply bending your wrist downward, to let the pole lift up as you ski forward. Do not try to prolong the pole plant by letting your arm fall behind your body. This will make your shoulders rotate through the turn and face uphill, which is something to be avoided.

The first step in turning, actually before the skis turn at all, is anticipation. As the skis and lower body proceed through the turn, your shoulders can remain facing downhill, without rotating at all. Your upper body isn't needed to complete the turn—it can be completed by the legs alone. By keeping your upper body facing downhill, you are automatically anticipating the next turn. When the present turn is complete you will be facing down the slope prepared to turn again. Thus, you have eliminated unnecessary actions, and the next turn can proceed sooner. On gentle, wide slopes, linking turns quickly is not too important. But on steep, narrow slopes, it can be essential. At times it can make the difference between getting down the slope and ending up in the trees.

Several reminders can help you keep your upper body facing downhill throughout the turn. Aiming your belly button downhill is one. Keeping your downhill shoulder back is another. This reminder may be helpful if you were taught to rotate your shoulders through the turn like a steering wheel. By telling yourself to keep the downhill shoulder back, you may be able to break this habit.

The primary reason for facing your upper body downhill after the turn has begun is to prepare for the next turn, but if you are turning slowly or traversing, it is not necessary to continue keeping your shoulders facing downhill. Let them face the ski tips—you will be more comfortable. However, when you are ready for the next turn, remember to anticipate with your shoulders *before* you turn.

An important exception to using anticipation is the "pure" carved turn which initiates the turn with edge change instead of foot twist. This is discussed in the next chapter.

Edging—Knee Angulation and Banking

Foot twist, to initiate a turn, is performed on flat skis. The skis should not be edged too early. Wait until the feet are reweighted. Once the feet and skis are reweighted, the turn is controlled by setting the edges of the skis into the slope. There are three ways of edging: knee and hip angulation and banking. Knee angulation and edge control have been discussed in several previous chapters.

As you begin to roll your knees uphill, the edges will start to grip the snow, but the skis will continue to slip sideways. By increasing the degree of knee angulation, lateral slippage of the edges is checked, and the skis will follow the direction of the tips (carving).

If you are unable to angulate the knees far enough to prevent slippage, it is often because your knee joints are too straight. You must flex them more by dropping your seat over your heels. Increased knee flexion permits a greater degree of knee angulation. These two actions, knee flexion and knee angulation, work together.

The second way of edging is by leaning your entire body inward, counteracting centrifugal force. Turning on skis is similar to an automobile turning on a highway. At high speeds, centrifugal force tends to pull the automobile off the highway. For this reason, high-speed roadways are often "banked" (tilted inward) in the direction of the turn to counteract centrifugal force. You too can "bank" turns by leaning your body inward, toward the center of the turn *(Figure 33).*

Banking sets the skis on their edges with much less effort than knee angulation. Banking can also edge the skis to a greater extent than knee angulation. However, banking can only be used while you are turning with some speed, because once the turn is completed, the centrifugal force will be dissipated. Thus, banking for edge control is limited to turns with some speed, while knee angulation provides edge control in all circumstances.

Learning edge control should start with knee angulation. As you begin to ski a little faster, you can try leaning your hips and upper body toward the center of your turn. As you bank, you will need less knee angulation to keep your edges biting into the slope. As you finish, you must straighten up your body and again use knee angulation for edge control. However, if you connect your turns so that the next turn begins as the last turn ends, your body may bank continuously from one side to the other in a smooth, rhythmical pattern. Banking is more applicable to carved turns because skidding often reduces speed to the point where banking cannot be used.

In summary, turns are completed when the skis are reweighted after unweighting. Both skis should carry some weight. The pole is released by bending the wrist down. Your shoulders should remain facing downhill when linking your turns. And your knees should angulate uphill to control your edges.

17 Skidding and Carving

All turns are completed by either skidding or carving (see Chapter 4). You should learn both techniques, as each is useful in different situations. Skidding is a way to brake as well as turn, whereas carving will permit you to maintain a comfortable speed without slowing down. Carving is the method racers use to avoid losing speed in their turns. This is described by Warren Witherell in *How the Racers Ski* (New York: W. W. Norton, 1972). However, if you're not a racer, you still want to learn to carve because it provides more control, takes less energy, gives you a smoother turn on packed snow, and is a necessity in powder.

Skidding

Skidding should be learned first because it is the main method of stopping and turning. Skidding begins as you reweight your feet after unweighting. At this point, your foot twist is slowing down, and your skis are lying fairly flat against the slope *(Figure 48).* Your skis will start to slide downhill in the direction of the fall line. To slow down, angulate your knees uphill, just enough to feel the edges of the skis begin to bite the snow. This maneuver is the same as sideslipping and will control your speed. However, you may want to continue turning. Do this by pushing your knees forward until you feel increasing pressure of your shins against your boot tops. This is *forward leverage,* which puts more weight on your ski tips and less on your tails, resulting in the tips digging into the slope while the tails pivot around the tips. To stop turning, shift your weight

Figure 48

Skidding

Skidding is completing a turn by sideslipping while the skis continue to rotate. The side of the ski leads the way through the turn, which leaves a wide track. Knee angulation controls the amount of edging needed to skid. On gentle slopes, the skis may lie flat against the hill, with no edging. On steep slopes, edging is needed to control the skid. In this example, minimal edging is needed, so no knee angulation is seen.

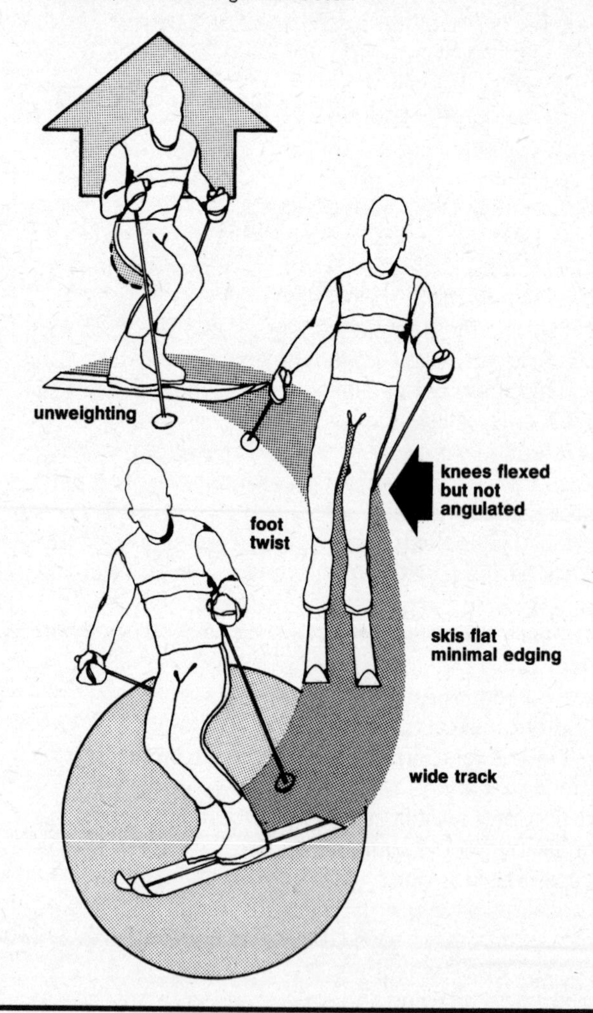

back to "center" or *neutral leverage,* and increase your edgeset. You are now ready for the next turn.

It is also possible to use rotation of your hips and shoulders to supply the turning force in a skidded turn. However, this results in your upper body facing uphill at the end of the turn, and it will require more time to begin the following turn. For this reason, it is best to avoid using upper body rotation for turning. Your goal should be to control your turns with your lower body, keeping your upper body as quiet as possible.

Traversing

Traversing is traveling across a hill perpendicular to the fall line. When truly at a right angle to the fall line, your skis will gradually slow down and stop. Therefore, to keep up your momentum, your skis must head a few degrees downhill.

In a traverse, your edges are set into the hill at enough of an angle to prevent sideslipping. The tips of the skis lead the direction while the rest of the ski follows the path of the tips. This is the simplest form of carving. To illustrate how the arc in the ski is used to turn, increase the edgeset of your skis while traversing a gentle slope. Do this by flexing your knees more and angulating them uphill. This will place the skis on their tips and tails, letting the center bend (see Chapter 3). The increased curve in the skis will gently turn you uphill. You can increase the degree of curve by pressing your knees forward and decrease it by putting more weight on your heels. Trying these maneuvers on a gentle slope is a good way to experience the feeling of carving.

Carving

Carving is following the path of the tips of your skis through a turn *(Figure 49).* It utilizes the same type of knee angulation as skidding, but more of it. In skidding, the knees adjust the degree of edging to *permit* slipping. In carving, the degree of edging must increase to *prevent* slipping. The edging is performed primarily by knee angulation but also by hip angulation and banking.

When carving, your speed is controlled by turning uphill. There is no sideslipping action to act as a brake. You decelerate by following the turn uphill; you accelerate by heading your skis downhill.

A sharper turn is achieved by increasing the arc in the ski, which can be done in several ways: increasing the degree of edgeset by increasing angulation; shifting most or all of your weight to one foot; stomping on your skis; extending your body (straightening up) or using forward leverage. Each of these actions will in-

Figure 49

Carving

Carving is completing a turn by following the direction of the curve of the edged skis. The tips of the skis lead the turn, which produces a narrower track than a skidded turn. The skis are edged either by knee angulation, as shown here, or by banking. Realistically, most carved turns contain an element of skidding. It is almost impossible to carve without a little lateral slippage. In practice, carved turns are those with minimal lateral slippage.

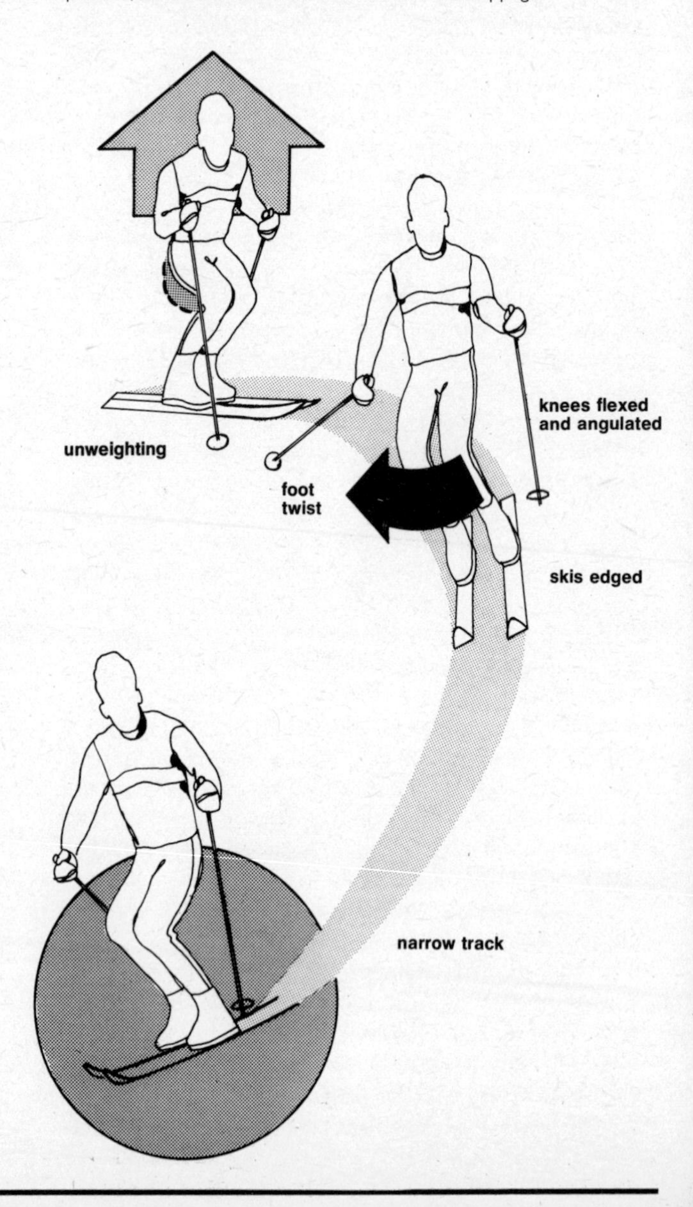

crease the reverse camber in your ski to form a tighter arc.

The "Pure" Carved Turn

The "pure" carved turn is a turn performed entirely on the edges of the skis. The bottoms of the skis never lie flat against the slope. The turn is initiated by an edge change, not a foot twist. It is completed by following the ski tips through the arc of the edged skis without sideslipping or skidding. The "pure" carved turn is a wider and more gradual turn than one performed with rotation. If you need a sharper turn, sharper than the carving ski can provide, you must use some form of rotation, either foot twist or skidding.

In truth, the "pure" carved turn is rarely performed. It is very difficult to turn without a minimal amount of sideslipping, although you should strive to keep these lateral movements to a minimum.

The basic skills used in carving are the same skills used in other parallel turns. However, some of them are used in different ways and need elaboration. These are: edge change, unweighting, anticipation, and leverage.

■ *Edge change*—rolling the edges from one side to the other—is the only way to initiate a "pure" carved turn. The edges must be set firmly enough to avoid sideslipping at the beginning of the turn. Once the skis begin to slip, more energy is required to check them and begin carving again. Edge change is performed either by angulating the knees or by banking from one side to the other.

■ *Unweighting* usually precedes edge change. Although it is possible to change edges without unweighting, a small amount of unweighting, for only a fraction of a second, is often needed to more easily release the previous edgeset. UP-unweighting may be used, but DOWN-unweighting or leg retraction can provide a smoother edge change and permit closer, continuous contact of the edges with the snow.

■ *Anticipation* is not a part of the pure carved turn. Turning the shoulders downhill, before the turn, is a form of rotation. It assists foot twisting, but will not aid edge changing. If you begin your turn with a foot twist and complete it with carving, anticipation is used. But if you initiate your turn with only an edge change, anticipation may interfere. When changing edges, the upper body and lower body turn together.

■ *Leverage* can affect the arc of the ski, but must be applied carefully. A small amount of forward weight transfer, by flexing the ankles a few degrees forward, increases the pressure on the front half of the ski, which is the more flexible half. This increases the arc in the ski and provides a tighter turn. It takes only a small amount of forward lean to increase the arc in the ski. If this action is exaggerated, the tail of the ski can unweight and begin to skid. Transferring weight toward the ski tip also introduces a slight braking effect.

Backward leverage, increasing the weight on the heels, takes the pressure off the ski tips and reduces the arc in the skis. This lengthens the radius of the turn. In general, long-radius turns are easier to perform without using leverage.

Skidding and carving are best practiced at a moderate speed on gentle slopes. However, the edge-controlling actions of knee flexion and knee angulation can be practiced standing still. Try it indoors, in front of a mirror. Observe that as you drop your seat lower, your knees can angulate to a greater degree sideways, thereby increasing the edgeset of your feet and skis. *It is not enough to simply flex your knees.* The main purpose of knee flexion is to loosen the knee joints so the knees can then angulate to the side. By concentrating your attention on your knees when skiing, you will soon begin to *feel* how the knees control your edges.

Wedeln is a series of quick, short turns closely linked together. The skier looks like he is wiggling down the slope, hence the name wedeln (German for wiggling). This chapter will discuss wedeln with the basic parallel turn described in Chapter 16. To differentiate this from other types of wedeln, this will be called simple wedeln. Simple wedeln uses the same basic skills as parallel turning. Nothing new is added except timing and rhythm. Each turn must be executed rapidly and immediately lead into the next turn.

Wedeln can be done with up-unweighting, down-unweighting, or leg retraction. However, it is easiest to learn to wedeln with up-unweighting. In this case, the sequence of actions is: 1) down 2) pole plant 3) up-unweight 4) foot twist or edge change and 5) minimal edging and skidding as you immediately drop down again to repeat the sequence. The shoulders anticipate the first turn, then remain facing downhill all the time. Only the lower body turns. The turns are short, seldom over 45 degrees to either side of the fall line. Turns are usually completed by skidding, but carving can also be used. Skidding or carving is performed simultaneously with the "down" preparation for the next turn. To wedeln smoothly, the actions must follow each other rhythmically, with precision and efficiency *(Figure 50).*

■ *Anticipation.* Keeping your upper body (head, shoulders, and hands) facing downhill is a vital part of wedeln. You can wedeln with your feet several inches apart, as long as you keep your upper body looking down the fall line. If you have never wedelned before, you should try wide-stance wedeln on a gentle slope. The only skills you need to begin wedeln are down-UP unweighting, foot twisting, and skidding. By trying to turn rapidly, you will realize why it is necessary to keep your upper body facing downhill all the time. If you let your upper body rotate with your turn, you will be unable to link your turns quickly.

■ *Down motion.* The down movement is the same preparatory down motion that was described for down-UP unweighting (see Chapter 16). However, when wedeln, the down motion must be very fast and be followed immediately by the UP motion.

■ *Edgeset.* In simple wedeln, there is very little edgeset. In this respect, simple wedeln differs from check-wedeln. Simple wedeln is used on gentle slopes where speed can be adequately controlled with a short skid after each turn. Check-wedeln is employed on steeper slopes where increased sideslipping and prolonged skidding are needed to reduce speed (see Chapter 19). In simple wedeln, there is no prolonged sideslip or skid at the end of the turn. However, there may be a small edgeset to stop a short skid. The edgeset occurs simultaneously with the pole plant.

■ *Pole plant.* In wedeln, just as in other turns, the pole plant occurs just prior to the UP motion. The proper moment is during the quick edgeset. The position of the pole plant is a little different than for slower turns. In wedeln, the pole is usually planted near the side of the boot or a little ahead of it. The pole plant is more a timing device than a support. Your weight is supported by the pole for a minimal period of time, if at all. Your arms should remain almost fixed, in front of your body. The pole is therefore placed at the most convenient spot to prevent much arm or shoulder movement. Thus, dropping the pole at your side will signal the UP motion, and the pole can immediately be lifted up again. You should not lean heavily on the pole; in wedeln you barely lean on it at all.

■ *Up motion.* The UP motion is a very quick return of your seat to its previous position without straightening your knees.

■ *Leverage.* Depending on how rapidly you wish to turn, you may transfer your weight forward to the balls of your feet, or you may keep your weight centered. During the skid, forward weight transfer partially unweights the tails, permitting them to pivot more rapidly around the tips. Use this when wedeln on steeper

Simple Wedeln

Figure 50

In simple wedeln, the upper body remains facing downhill all the time, so it is always in a position of anticipation. The down motion is followed immediately by the pole plant and the UP motion to unweight. While unweighted, a quick foot twist and/or edge change occur. The turn is finished with a minimal skid or carve, which is accompanied by the down motion for the next turn.

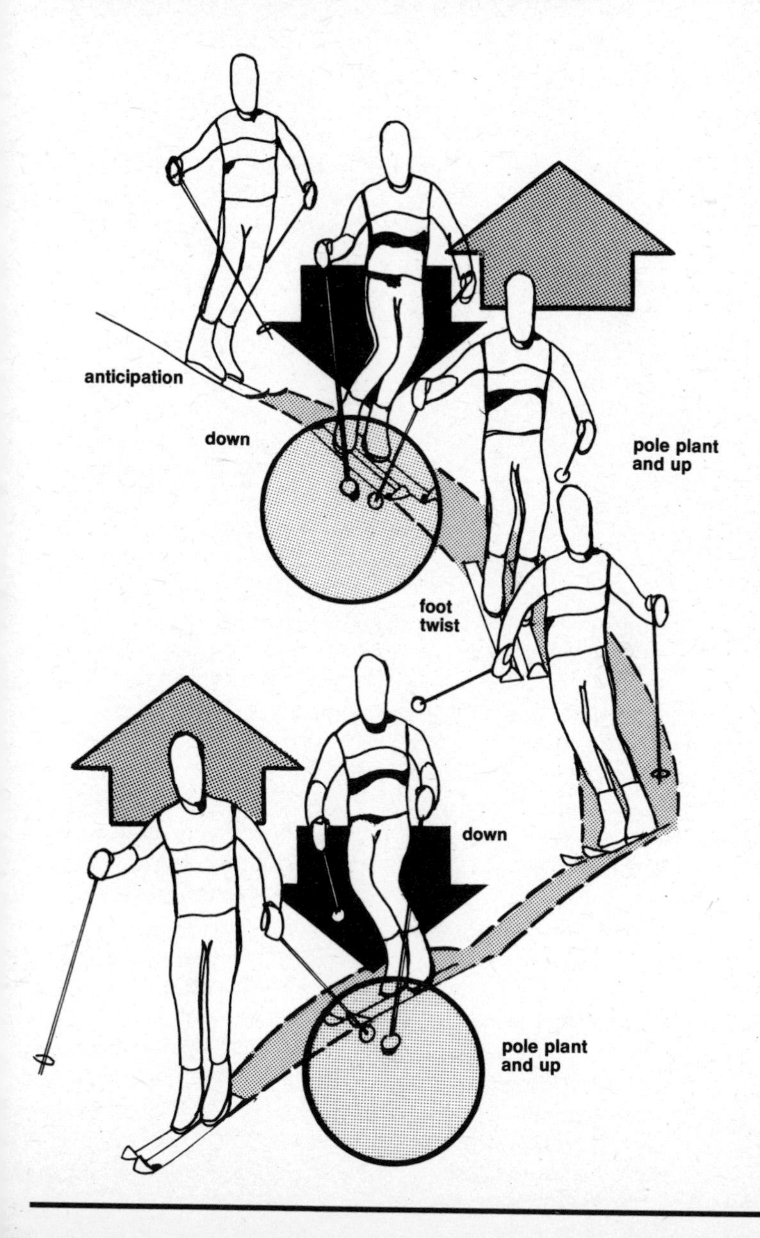

slopes. On gentle slopes where minimal skidding is needed, your weight may remain evenly distributed between the balls and heels of your feet. When wedeln in deep powder forward leverage cannot be used at all.

19 Checking and Check-Wedeln

Checking is suddenly stopping your sideslip. It is performed by quickly angulating your knees uphill to increase your edgeset.

Checking When Sideslipping

Learning to check is a part of learning to sideslip. On a moderately steep slope, begin a controlled sideslip by deangulating your knees. Then check the sideslip by angulating them back uphill *(Figure 45)*. Three points should be observed: 1) knee flexion is essential to permit knee angulation; 2) knee angulation is the action which does the checking; and 3) your weight should be centered on your feet, with pressure felt against your boot tops and your heels. The heel pressure is important because it prevents the tails from skidding.

Checking When Traversing (Garlands)

Slowing down from a traverse is done by checking. This is easier to learn by traversing a smooth, gentle slope. To check, first start your skis sideslipping by rolling your flexed knees away from the hill. Your skis will begin to sideslip while still moving forward. Once the sideslip has started, check it by angulating your knees back into the hill. This will stop your lateral movement and slow down your forward speed. If you continue to press your knees uphill, your forward movement will also stop. But if you quickly let your knees move away from the hill the instant your sideslip is checked, your forward momentum can continue in another traverse at a lower level on the hill. Continue this exercise, all the way across the hill: traverse, deangulate your knees, sideslip, then angulate them back. Do this with both small and large degrees of knee flexion. You will notice that it is easier to maintain your balance and control your knee angulation from lower body positions with more knee flexion. With a little practice, you will start to feel how checking can be used to stop all lateral motion and reduce forward speed. The turns in this exercise are called garlands, because of the tracks they leave in the snow *(Figure 51).*

Checking Before Turning — Platform — Rebound — Pre-turn

Checking is often used to reduce speed just before turning. If you are able to check while traversing, you can now try to check before turning (check-turn). Beginning from a sideslip with anticipation, the sequence of actions is: 1) down 2) check and 3) up-unweight. This is similar to the down-UP motion discussed for parallel turns in Chapter 16, with some modifications. The down motion is emphasized by dropping your seat quite low, and it is prolonged by adding a check. Angulate your knees uphill until the edges bite. Your ankles should not flex too far forward; keep your heels weighted. Plant your pole just as your sideslip is checked. Plant it in line with your feet, a comfortable distance downhill.

Up-unweighting follows immediately, and almost automatically. The combination of tight knee flexion and knee angulation stretches the thigh muscles to the point where they are uncomfortably lengthened and anxious to shorten. As soon as you stop stretching and begin to lift up, the muscles shorten, the legs partially straighten, and your seat rises. Your feet will become weightless, and may even leave the ground if you lift up vigorously. The position of tight compression of the legs when checking provides a springboard from which to launch a turn. This position is called a *platform.*

The force to up-unweight is greater in a check-turn than in a simple parallel turn. The extra power comes from potential energy which builds up in the stretched thigh muscles. The "checking" position tightly compresses the lower body, like squeezing a rubber ball:

Garlands

Figure 51

Traverse, sideslip, and check. Beginning from a traverse with the knees flexed, the knees roll downhill to flatten the skis and begin a sideslip. The sideslip is checked by knees rolling back uphill to re-edge the skis.

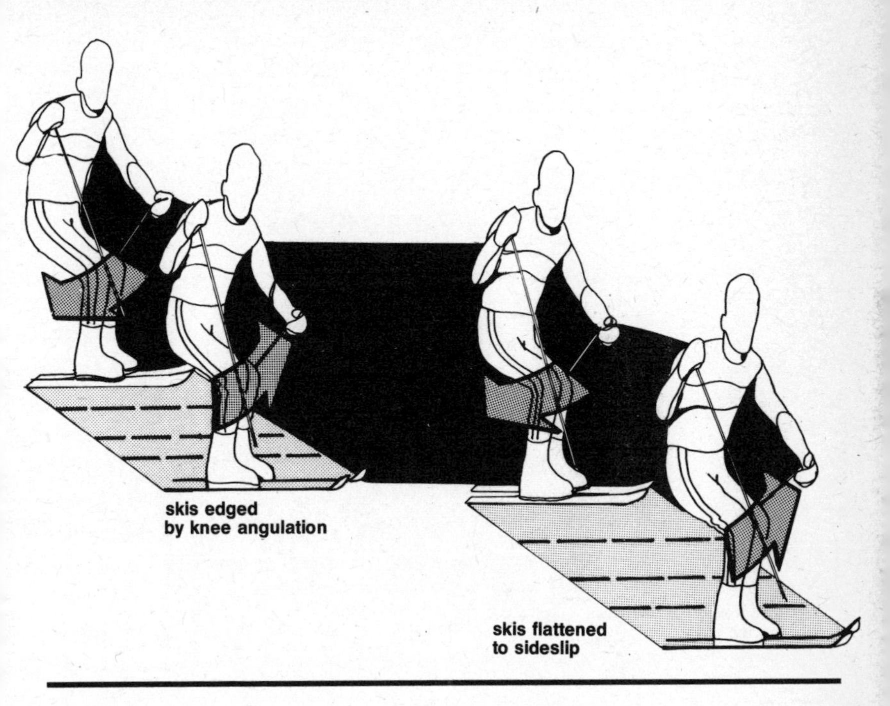

When the ball is released, the rubber rebounds. Similarly, when the stretched muscles are released, the lower body rebounds. This *rebound* is usually strong enough to unweight your feet, without requiring additional efforts on your part. By simply relaxing your leg muscles just after your pole is planted, you will permit the rebound to lift the weight from your feet *(Figure 52).*

The checking action will usually turn the skis slightly uphill, just before turning. For this reason, checking before turning is sometimes referred to as a *pre-turn* or *counter-turn.*

Check-Wedeln (Short-Swing)

Adding a prolonged sideslip and a check to simple wedeln results in check-wedeln. On steep slopes, checking is often needed for speed control. The combination of anticipation and checking puts enough stretch on the abdominal and leg extensor muscles

Figure 52

Check-Wedeln

Check-wedeln utilizes a prolonged sideslip and check before each turn. Begin with anticipation. The down motion is prolonged by angulating the knees uphill at the end of the down motion. This tightens the leg muscles as the lower body prepares to lift up. The pole is planted and the stretched leg muscles rebound by springing the body up. While unweighted, the feet are easily twisted to face downhill and continue to turn across the fall line. In this example, the turn is completed by skidding.

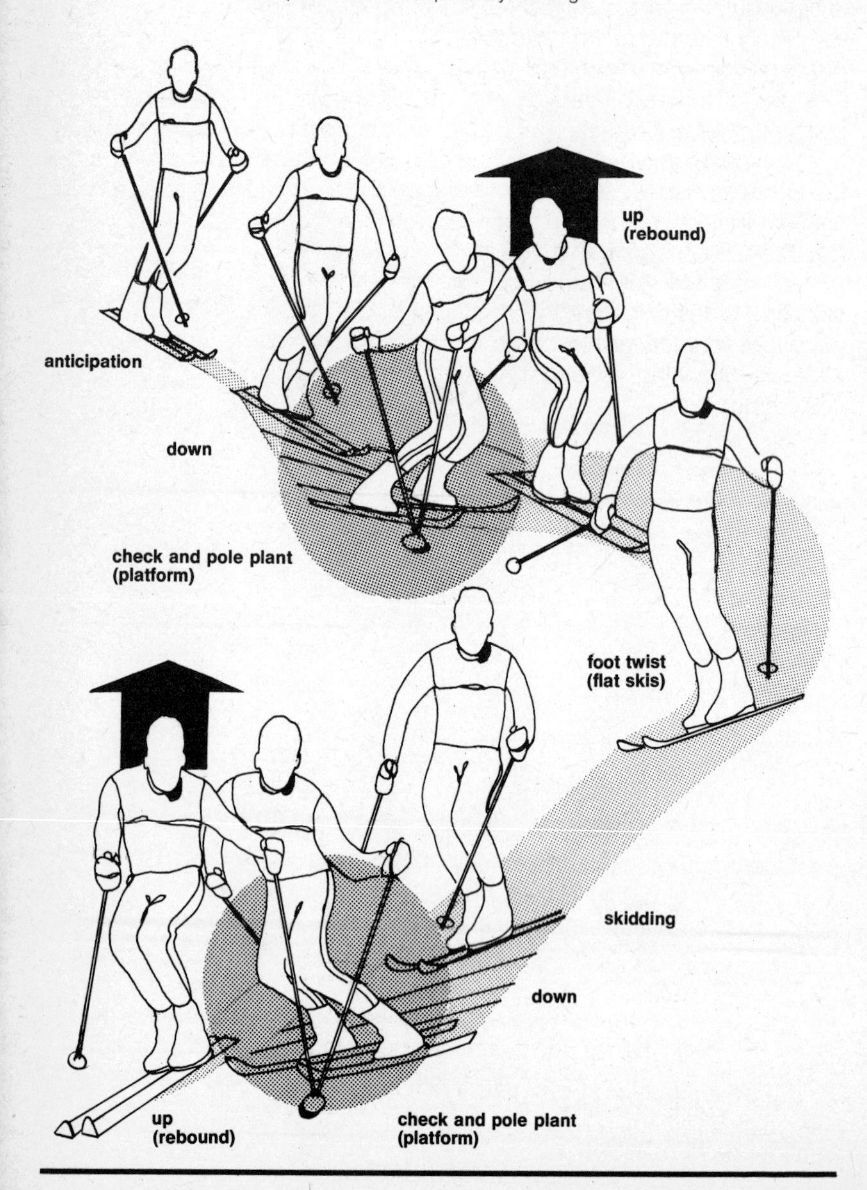

that your skis rotate as soon as you rebound. Almost automatically your feet will face downhill. The rotation is usually so fast that the momentum continues to pivot your skis past the fall line to point them across the hill. As you reweight your skis, you will be skidding. Control your skid and reduce your speed by edging with knee angulation. You are now ready to begin your next turn with the same "down-check-up" rhythm.

Forward Leverage

The use of forward leverage with check-wedeln will permit tighter and quicker turns. Apply forward leverage by pushing your knees forward just after your heels have pushed you up to unweight. As your skis are reweighted, the tips will grab the slope first, permitting the tails to continue pivoting. As the turn is completed, recenter your weight, thereby changing your skid to a sideslip before the next turn. Remembering to correct your forward leverage is important, because effective checking requires considerable weight on your heels.

Jetting

Jetting is a quick thrust of the feet forward as a result of releasing the stretched leg extensor muscles. These muscles are stretched by flexing the knees and are further stretched by knee angulation and leg retraction *(Figure 22).* In each case, the legs are tightly compressed. At the instant of unweighting, the same rebounding force which unweights the body *upward* in a check-turn is partially diverted to thrust the feet *forward* in a jet-turn.

Two actions are used to convert the sharp check-turn into a smoother jet-turn. First, the abrupt checking action is softened by altering the timing of the down motion with knee angulation. To produce the sharp edgeset of a check-turn, *first* flex your knees, *then* angulate them into the hill. To reduce the abruptness and perform a smoother turn, simultaneously flex and angulate your knees. The difference between these two rhythms is subtle, but important. When flexing your knees, you are also dropping your seat and partially down-unweighting. This reduces the pressure on your skis. If down-unweighting accompanies knee angulation, the edges cannot bite as sharply, making the edgeset softer and lessening the rebound. Second, rebound upward is limited by completely relaxing your legs at the moment of unweighting and keeping your shoulders the same distance from the slope. By preventing the shoulders from lifting up, the rebounding force will push the knees upward, toward the chest.

This takes all pressure off the skis and permits the stretched extensor muscles to jet the feet forward.

Jetting is only one element of a turn. "Jet-turns" are turns which include jetting. They can be performed with up-unweighting or leg retraction. The "classical" jet-turn uses up-unweighting and is similar to a check-turn but smoother. Avalement also uses jetting and will be discussed in Chapter 22.

Jet-Turn

The jet-turn described below is the classical jet-turn as just defined *(Figure 53).* It includes the following elements, in sequence:

1) anticipation
2) knee angulation simultaneously with a down motion
3) pre-turn and edgeset
4) pole plant
5) up-unweighting—relaxing the leg muscles and keeping the shoulders down
6) automatic thrusting of the feet forward (jetting)
7) letting the upper body pivot the feet
8) inward body lean (banking)
9) completing the turn by carving, skidding, or both

The jetting action is automatic—the skier relaxes his muscles, and the jetting occurs spontaneously. You should not consciously push your feet forward. If your muscles are stretched far enough during the preparatory actions, jetting will "happen" when you unweight. Thus, the preliminary motions are the most important features of a jet-turn. If these are performed properly, the turn proceeds automatically.

■ *Anticipation* is an essential part of a jet-turn, just as it is in simple wedeln and check-wedeln. This is the rotational force which pivots your skis during unweighting *(Figure 27).*

Increasing *knee angulation* just prior to unweighting increases your edgeset and turns the skis slightly uphill (pre-turn, Chapter 19).

In check-wedeln, the pre-turn is primarily a sideslip, with a slight rotation of the skis uphill (skidding). In the jet-turn, the softer edgeset lets the skis move forward (carving) as well as move sideways (skidding). The edgeset is softened even further in avalement by tilting the upper body downhill during the pre-turn (Chapter 22).

The *pre-turn* is performed with the upper body fac-

Figure 53

Jet-Turn

The jet-turn begins with anticipation. Knee flexion (the down motion) and knee angulation occur together. The pole is planted and up-unweighting follows. But instead of rebounding straight up as in check-wedeln, the legs relax and the upper body is prevented from rising up. The rebounding force is thereby diverted to push the knees upward and jet the feet forward. Only then do the feet pivot into the turn and face downhill. The slight delay in the foot twist results in the upper body's leaning inward, in a position for banking.

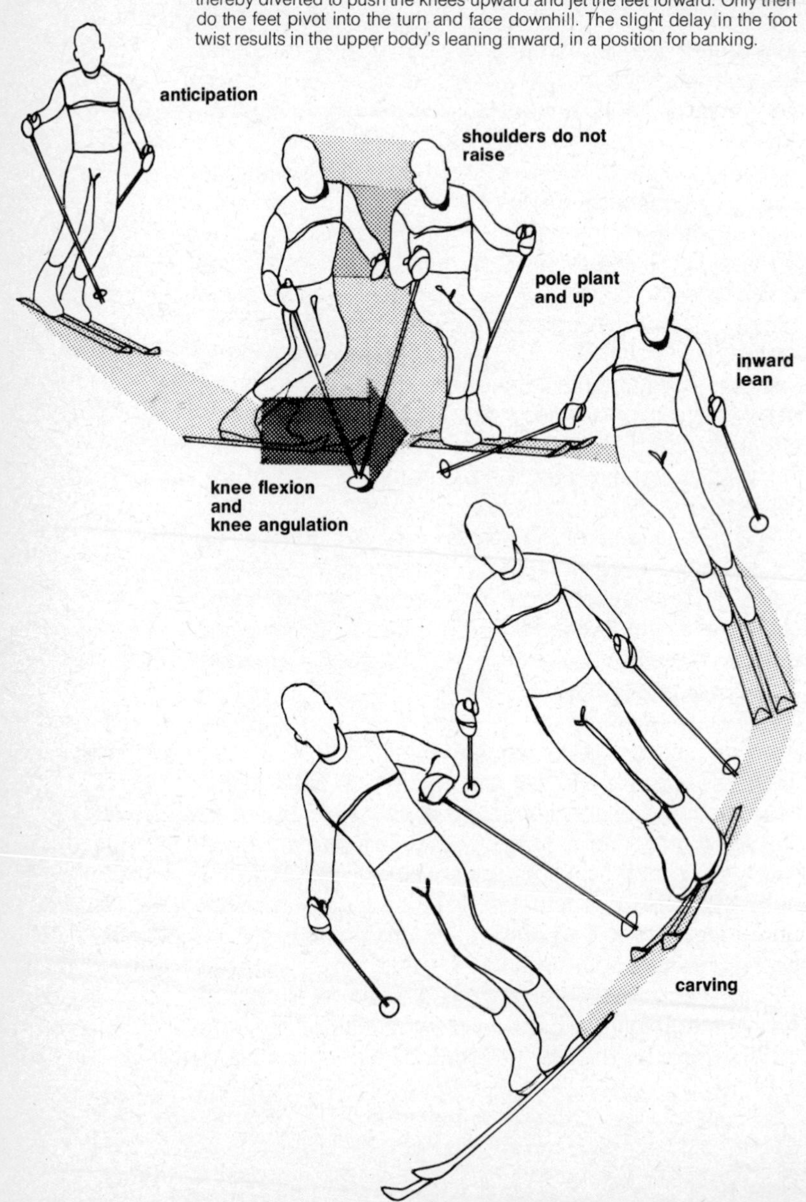

ing downhill in the position of anticipation. Thus, the pre-turn stretches further the already stretched abdominal and back muscles, so the turning force of anticipation will be even stronger during unweighting.

The *pole plant* occurs at the end of the pre-turn and signals the beginning of up-unweighting. As you suddenly relax your legs and keep your shoulders down, the rebound force lifts your knees and advances your feet forward. An instant later, your feet begin to pivot downhill.

Jetting the feet forward accounts for the main difference between the check-turn and the classical jet-turn. In the check-turn, the feet pivot directly underneath the body, while in the jet-turn, because the feet are first thrust forward and then pivot, the feet twist outside the line of the body. This places the body on a slant, leaning inward toward the center of the turn (banking). From the position of inward lean, the turn can be completed like any other parallel turn, with carving, skidding, or both. Forward leverage can be used in jet-turns in the same way it was used in check-turns (Chapter 19).

The smoothness of the jet-turn can be attributed to softening the edgeset before unweighting, and assuming a position for banking early in the turn. Because one of its features is banking, which cannot be done at slow speeds, the jet-turn is used at moderate or high speeds.

Difference Between Simple Wedeln, Check-Wedeln, and Jet-Turn Wedeln

All three use down-UP unweighting and anticipation. In simple wedeln, the feet twist under the body to initiate the turn. In check-wedeln, a check is added to the down motion of simple wedeln. This adds the element of compression or stretching of the extensor muscles. The rebound that follows is used to up-unweight in check-wedeln. In jet-turns, the same rebound is used both to thrust the feet forward and to up-unweight. Thus, in check-wedeln, the feet begin to turn immediately on the up motion, while in jet-turns there is a delay. The feet first jet forward and then turn.

Bumps and moguls present their own challenge. They require more strength, energy, and skill to maintain good balance and constant edge control. The size of a mogul is an important factor in turning. The larger the mogul, the more difficult the turn. Techniques which work on small moguls may be less effective on large ones. Similarly, speed and snow conditions can affect turning. Therefore, the accomplished skier should have several methods from which to choose.

Absorbing Moguls — Knee Action

While traversing a bumpy slope, you go up and down many moguls. If your knees remain in the same position of flexion, you feel increased pressure against your skis as you go up the mogul and a sudden loss of pressure as you go down it. This constant variation in pressure against your skis makes bumpy slopes more difficult to master than smooth ones. However, by proper use of your knees, you can absorb the bumps and minimize their unstabilizing effects.

Flexing your knees unweights your feet, thereby momentarily reducing the pressure of the hill against your skis. Standing up (leg extension) produces the reverse effect, increasing the pressure against your skis. Therefore, by flexing your knees as you ascend a mogul and extending them as you descend, you can neutralize the effects of the slope, and the pressure against the skis remains constant. Practice absorbing moguls by traversing back and forth across a bumpy slope. Practice this until your knees automatically flex and extend over moguls without your consciously thinking about it *(Figure 54)*.

As you go uphill, the hill tends to throw your body

Absorbing Bumps

Figure 54

Going up a bump, bend (flex) your knees; and going down, straighten them out (extend). This maintains an even pressure of the skis against the slope. In addition, lean slightly forward when ascending and slightly backward when descending the bump.

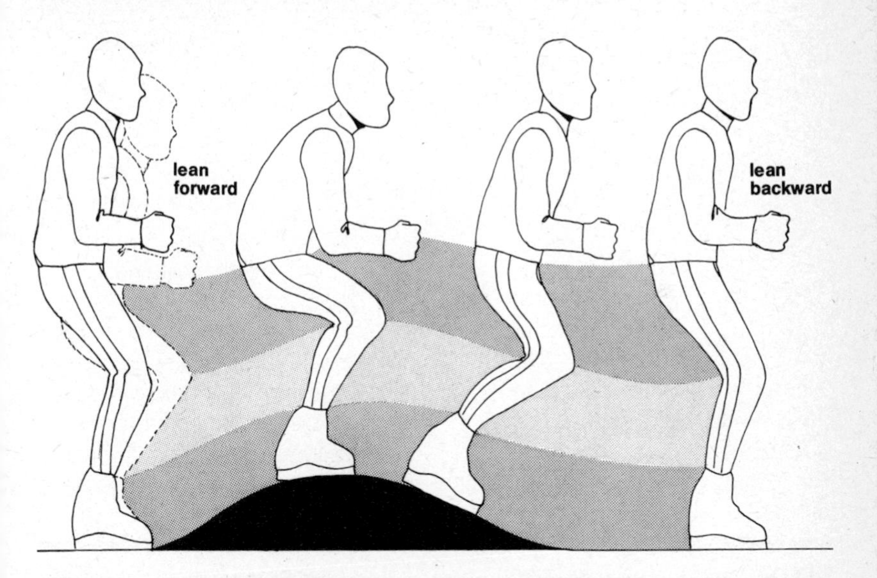

backward. Counteract this force by leaning forward as you ascend a mogul. Similarly, on the downside of the mogul your body is drawn forward. Balance this by leaning *slightly* backward. Both of these changes, forward and backward lean, are subtle weight shifts, which, if exaggerated, cause loss of balance.

Turning on a Mogul

Any method that is used for turning on a smooth slope can be used on a bumpy one. However, those techniques which include the principles of knee flexion and extension to absorb the moguls will work better than those that do not.

Turning Without Unweighting

■ *Stem turns* on moguls and in mogul fields should be avoided. Stemming at the crest of a mogul can be dangerous, as an abrupt edgeset by a stemmed ski can cause straightening of the stemmed leg and loss of control. Stemming in the trough between the moguls is not good either because there is no room to spread the tails of the skis. If a stem is used on a mogul, it

Figure 55

Unweighting by a Mogul

From a traverse, begin by ascending a mogul in a fairly upright position. Anticipate by facing your shoulders downhill. Flex your knees slowly as you approach the crest. Plant the pole at the crest, when the body is in a tucked position. As the skis pass the crest they automatically unweight. Immediately twist your feet and slowly extend your legs to maintain pressure against the downside of the mogul.

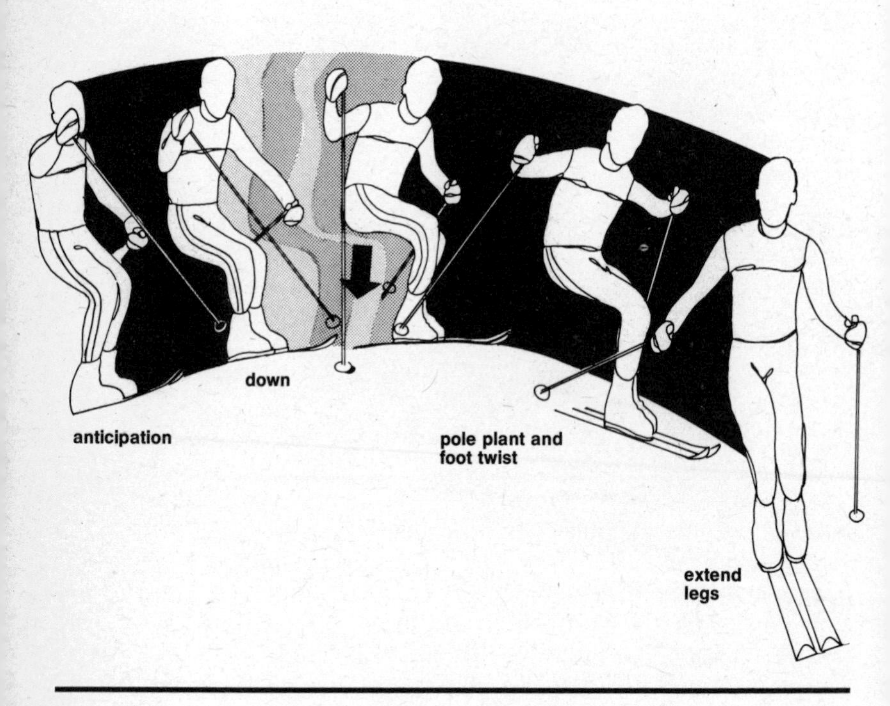

should only be at slow speeds with minimal edgeset by the stemmed ski.

■ *Parallel turns* can be performed on moguls without actively unweighting. As mentioned in Chapter 5, when you ski over the crest of a mogul your feet are automatically unweighted by the slope falling away. If you twist your feet just as they pass the peak of the mogul, they will turn. The fact that your tips and tails are suspended in air will let them turn more easily. The turn can be facilitated by flexing your knees on the way up, planting your downhill pole as you reach the crest, turning your shoulders downhill before you turn (anticipation), and extending your legs as you turn onto

Knees Flexed on Mogul Crest

Figure 56

Flexed knees on the crest of a mogul provide a variety of choices for turning. If you are traveling with moderate speed, your feet can rotate without unweighting. At slow speeds, either down-unweight or use leg retraction. To down-unweight, drop your seat quickly at the crest. Perform leg retraction by lowering your seat before you reach the crest and pulling your knees upwards at the crest. In order to maintain balance, it is necessary to bend forward at the waist at the moment you lift your knees. The pole plant is used for balance and stability during unweighting. (Photo by David Sanders.)

the downside of the mogul *(Figure 55)*. The turn is completed like any other turn, with skidding, carving, or both. Letting a mogul unweight your feet is more effective at fast speeds than at slow speeds. When traveling slowly, a more active form of unweighting is needed *(Figure 56)*.

Turning with Unweighting

Up-unweighting, down-unweighting, and leg retraction can assist in turning on moguls. Of these, up-unweighting is the least desirable for the reasons discussed below.

■ *Up-unweighting* on moguls can be used to learn the feeling of weightlessness. By performing a quick down-UP motion at the crest of a mogul, you will be completely unweighted—you may even be airborne. However, it takes considerable time and distance on the downside of the mogul to control your speed. While unweighted, there is ample time to twist your feet and perform your turn. The problem occurs as your skis contact the snow on the downside because they will have trouble edging. Since the slope is moving away from your skis, it is difficult to put weight and pressure on your edges. Because your knees are almost straight from your up-motion, you are unable to adequately angulate your knees. Furthermore, as you flex your knees to permit more knee angulation, you are also down-unweighting, which continues to minimize the pressure your edges can exert on the snow. As a result, your skis sideslip rapidly, without control, for several feet. Eventually, you will feel enough weight on your feet to be able to gradually check your speed. Once your knees are flexed again, you can increase the pressure on your edges by extending your knees.

The disadvantage of up-unweighting over moguls is the loss of control on the downhill side. The prolonged period of unweighting gives the skis too much time to accelerate before enough pressure builds up on their edges to decelerate. The steeper the mogul, the more difficult up-unweighting becomes. It should now be apparent that instead of lifting up on top of a mogul it is better to simply twist your feet without actively trying to unweight, as described in the previous section. Another approach is to down-unweight.

■ *Down-unweighting,* unlike up-unweighting, permits early pressure of the skis against the downside of the slope. One way to get the feeling of down-unweighting is to stand erect on the crest of a mogul, preferably a steep one. The tips and tails of your skis are suspended in air as you face across the hill. Begin with anticipation, facing your shoulders downhill. Next, plant your downhill pole one and a half to two feet below your boot. As you plant the pole, your upper body starts to drift downhill. Don't try to stop it. Instead, maintain your balance with the pole and quickly drop your seat. Your feet will begin to pivot downhill, and your skis will descend the back side of the mogul, still in contact with the snow *(Figure 57).*

It is now easy to complete your turn. Your feet are al-

Down-Unweighting on a Mogul

Figure 57

To down-unweight, stand on top of a mogul with your skis facing across the hill. Begin by facing the shoulders downhill (anticipation). Next, plant the downhill pole about two feet from your boot. As the body begins to tilt forward, suddenly and quickly flex your knees and drop your seat. Your feet will be pulled downhill into the turn. Complete the turn by skidding, carving, or both (steering). During completion, slowly extend (straighten) your legs.

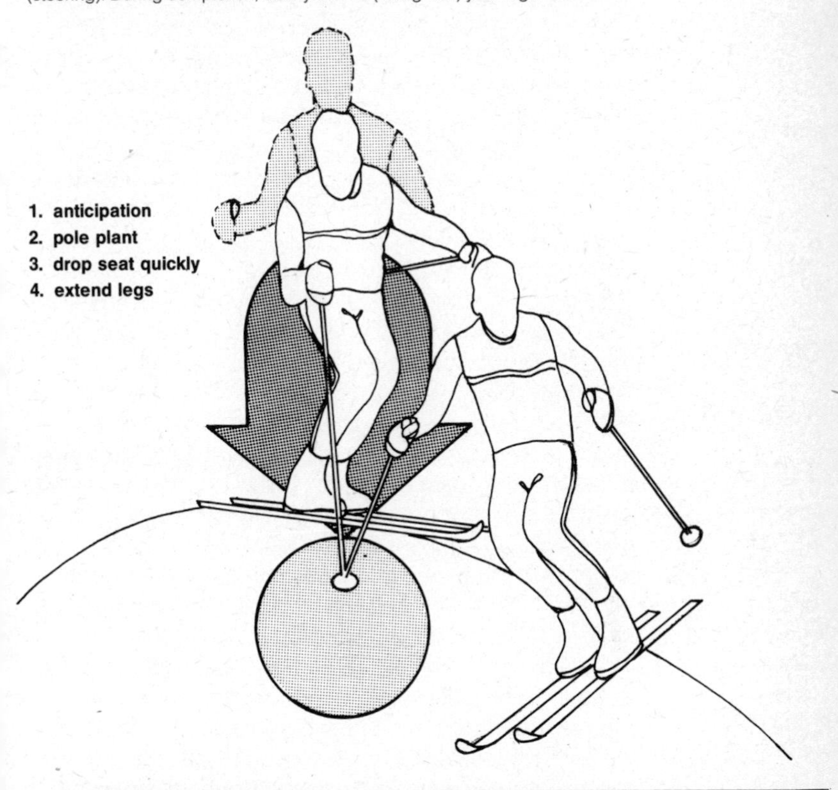

ready partially weighted and your knees flexed. Hold this position, with your skis relatively flat, to permit your skis to rotate past the fall line and begin to turn uphill. Then angulate your knees into the hill to control your skid or carve. At the same time, extending your knees will put even more pressure on your skis for additional edge control. It also gets you in the proper position to drop down on the next mogul.

Once you can down-unweight from one mogul, repeat the process at the crest of another without stopping. As you begin up the mogul, your body should be fairly upright. Anticipate before reaching the crest. A couple of feet before the peak, plant your pole, then flex your knees quickly. Keep your weight centered as you down-unweight by dropping your seat over your heels, not behind them. Avoid the common tendency of placing too much weight on your heels and losing your balance.

Down-unweighting on moguls is reserved for turns at slower speeds. At fast speeds, it can be replaced by the mogul's doing the unweighting, as described in the previous section. The difference between the two is the speed of lowering the seat. The knees flex quickly when down-unweighting and more gradually when the mogul does the unweighting.

■ *Leg retraction* is the fastest technique for unweighting. The muscle actions were described in Chapter 5 as lifting your legs up from a flexed position. Leg retraction is often preceded by a preliminary down motion, but if your knees are already well flexed, a down motion is not essential.

To leg retract on moguls, begin by ascending the mogul with your body in a fairly upright position. About three feet from the crest 1) anticipate 2) plant your pole far ahead of your boot and 3) drop your seat down over your heels. You are now ready to leg retract. As you reach the crest simultaneously tighten your abdominal muscles, lift your knees up, and bend slightly forward at the waist. As you unweight, your body is tightly compressed, more so than with down-unweighting. This lasts but a fraction of a second as your legs rebound downward, automatically extending your knees. This very early extension permits the skis to almost immediately exert pressure on the backside of the mogul. It is this feature of early, automatic extension that makes leg retraction an excellent technique for controlling big moguls at high speeds. It permits the skis to be pressing against the slope almost all the time. However, because leg retraction is so fast, it unweights for a small fraction of a second. It cannot be used at slow speeds because the skis will be reweighted before an effective turn begins.

During unweighting by leg retraction, turns are initiated by either foot twist or edge change. Foot twist is the simplest turn, and can be assisted by anticipation. Combining leg retraction with an early edge change is discussed under avalement, Chapter 22.

Moguls Versus Smooth Slopes

Down-Unweighting and Leg Retraction

Just as down-unweighting and leg retraction provide better-controlled turns on moguls, they can also provide well-controlled and faster turns on smooth slopes. To learn down-unweighting and leg retraction, begin on moguls where the period of unweighting is prolonged on the downside of the mogul. This makes it easier to *feel* the action. On moguls, down and up movements are used both to absorb the bumps and to unweight. Once you've learned these techniques on moguls, you can try them on smooth slopes. Here, they are used for unweighting only, so less vertical motion is needed and faster turns are possible.

Down-unweighting on smooth slopes begins with the knees slightly flexed. Start by planting your pole and immediately dropping your seat over your heels. During the moment of unweighting, either twist your feet or change your edges. When using foot twist to initiate your turn, precede the down motion with anticipation. On the other hand, edge change does not require anticipation (Chapter 17). Finish the turn by carving or skidding and extending your legs. Leg extension provides delicate edge control for completing the turn.

Down-unweighting requires only a fraction of a second to unweight. However, it takes longer to reweight the skis and extend the legs in preparation for the next turn. For this reason, down-unweighting works best at slower speeds.

At fast speeds, leg retraction is more effective because it not only unweights the legs instaneously but also reweights and extends them very quickly. With leg retraction, the legs reweight and extend almost automatically. To leg retract on smooth slopes, begin with your knees and ankles moderately flexed. Unweight by planting your pole, quickly tightening your abdominal muscles, and lifting your thighs upward. Raise your legs just enough to take the weight off your feet and flex slightly forward from the waist, to keep your weight centered. During the short instant of unweighting, the skis are flattened, then twisted and/or re-edged. Reweighting and leg extension occur by relaxing the tensed thigh muscles, thereby permitting the legs to rebound quickly and be ready for the next turn.

Leg retraction on smooth slopes requires minimal vertical motion. The leg muscles tighten and relax with so little up and down movement that this can be called isometric contraction (muscle tightening without motion). It is this economy of movement that makes it possible to wedeln very rapidly with leg retraction.

22

Avalement

The word avalement comes from the French word *avaler,* meaning to swallow. Avalement is a method for turning smoothly over moguls by "swallowing" or absorbing the bumps. It combines the basic elements of leg retraction, jetting, and early edging by banking. Thus, avalement is a jet-turn which employs leg retraction to unweight.

Avalement is easiest to learn by first learning the "classical" jet-turn (Chapter 20) and leg retraction (Chapter 21). There are several similarities between jet-turns and avalement:

1) Both use anticipation.

2) Both turns are preceded by a pre-turn, which combines a down motion with increased knee angulation (and leg compression).

3) In both turns, at the moment of unweighting the feet are thrust forward (jetted) and then begin to turn.

4) In both turns, the body leans inward after jetting so the turns can be completed with edging by banking.

Avalement differs from the "classical" jet-turn in the following ways:

1) The pole is planted earlier in avalement, near the beginning of the down motion and the pre-turn.

2) During the down motion of avalement, the upper body begins to tilt downhill. This minimizes the abrupt checking potential of the pre-turn.

3) In avalement, unweighting is by active leg retraction, rather than by passive leg relaxation and rebounding upward.

4) In avalement, very early leg extension maintains good snow contact on the back side of the mogul.

Avalement is easiest to learn on moguls. Later it can

be used on smooth slopes. The actions occur in rapid sequence, beginning in a traverse position up the side of a mogul *(Figure 58)*:

1) keeping the body fairly upright
2) anticipate
3) pole plant—about three feet from the crest
4) pre-turn—simultaneously
  a) tilting the upper body downhill
  b) using knee flexion
  c) using knee angulation uphill
5) unweighting at the crest of the mogul by leg retraction
6) automatic jetting of the feet forward
7) letting the upper body pivot the feet into the turn
8) edging the skis by banking
9) extending the legs throughout the turn
10) completing the turn by carving, skidding, or both

As you go up a mogul, your legs are probably extended from completing the previous turn. If not, partially straighten them to permit some room for a down motion as you ascend the mogul. Anticipation will be automatic if you have been keeping your shoulders facing downhill all the time. An extreme degree of anticipation is not necessary, particularly if you do not wish a tight turn. Anticipation can be delayed until you plant your pole. The pole plant signals the beginning of the turn. The pole is planted a comfortable distance ahead of your downhill foot.

As soon as your pole is planted, tilt your shoulders downhill on a line between your skis and your pole plant. This is a gentle action. If you plunge downhill, your skis will not have time to jet forward as you unweight. Tilt your body by simply relaxing your back muscles. In the down motion during the pre-turn, drop your seat over your heels to keep the weight centered. Avoid sitting back with more than half your weight on your heels.

During the down motion your knees not only flex but also angulate uphill, as if performing a check. The down motion and the early tilt of the body downhill minimize the edgeset and help the skis carve a pre-turn with minimal lateral slippage.

At precisely the crest of the mogul retract your legs. During the moment of unweighting that follows, your feet should automatically jet forward, still slightly on

Avalement

Figure 58

Begin avalement by ascending a mogul with the body fairly upright and the shoulders facing downhill (anticipation). Plant the downhill pole ahead of the foot. Immediately pre-turn by flexing and angulating the knees while letting the upper body start to fall downhill. As the feet pass the pole's basket, tighten your abdominal muscles, lift your legs, and flex your waist. The skis will automatically jet forward, then flatten, twist downhill, and roll onto their inside edges. The body is now leaning inward, prepared to bank the completion of the turn.

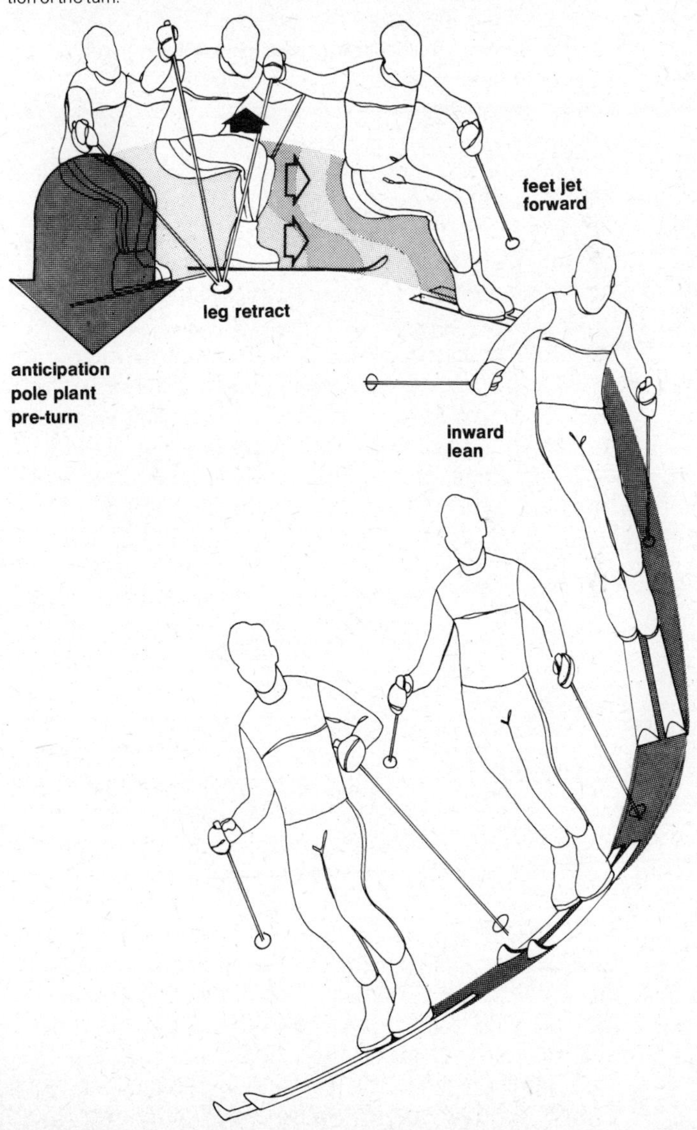

their uphill edges. Within an instant, your skis will be flattened by the pull of your upper body, which is already moving downhill. While flat, the skis can be twisted before they continue their edge change. Or the skis may change edges without a foot twist. In either case, the turn is completed by carving, although some skidding may accompany it. Leg extension also takes place on the downside of the mogul. The next turn can now be approached with minimal lateral slippage in a fairly upright position.

Down-Unweighting Instead of Leg Retraction

The basic elements in avalement are:

1) approaching the turn with a carved pre-turn and minimal sideslipping
2) unweighting by leg retraction
3) jetting the feet forward
4) delaying turning the feet downhill—first the upper body moves downhill, then the feet
5) early banking for edging

In summary, avalement differs from the classical jet-turn by minimizing sideslipping before the turn and by using leg retraction instead of up-unweighting. This allows greater snow contact throughout the turn and accounts for the elegance and grace of the turn.

Part III

Cross-Country Skiing

23

Principles of Cross-Country Skiing

More than four thousand years ago people in the Arctic Circle discovered that skis were a better way of traveling through snow than snowshoes. For centuries the Scandinavians used cross-country skis as a means of transportation. It has only been in the past one hundred years that cross-country (Nordic) skiing has become an activity for recreation as well as a way of traveling.

Nordic skiing is quite easy to learn because it is essentially walking on skis. Almost anyone who can walk can cross-country ski. However, while most Nordic skiing is performed on flat terrain, there are often a few hills to ascend and descend along the route. It is to negotiate these hills that the cross-country skier must develop some of the same skills as the downhill skier.

The principles of cross-country (Nordic) and downhill (Alpine) skiing are quite similar. They both are based on the ability to travel over snow with long boards strapped to the feet. The goal is the same: learning to control the skis resting on the snow. Whether you are using downhill or cross-country skis, the actions of the skis are only four: edging, balancing, rotating, and unweighting.

In downhill skiing, rotating and unweighting are needed to perform quick parallel turns. In cross-country skiing, parallel turns are rarely used. As a result, Nordic skiing is easier to learn than downhill skiing because edging and balancing are the only skills to master.

In cross-country skiing, edging is used for climbing, stopping, and turning. Effective edging requires flexing the knees and rolling them sideways. These actions are the same as those used in downhill skiing (Chapter 1, *Figures 1 and 2*).

Balance, the second basic skill, is a little easier to learn in cross-country skiing because it involves the coordination of knee and ankle flexion only (Chapter 2, *Figures 5 and 6*).

Walking and Gliding

Walking over flat terrain is the primary action in cross-country skiing, while turning is the main activity in downhill skiing. For this reason, the equipment for each sport is designed differently. The thin skis, soft, flexible boots, and free-heel bindings used in cross-country skiing were designed to permit easy walking and longer gliding. Unfortunately, there is a disadvantage to these features. Stopping and turning are more difficult to perform on cross-country skis because the heel is not fixed to the ski.

Whether you are walking on downhill or cross-country skis, the actions are the same. One ski slides forward, then the other. The poles are very helpful when walking. In the one-pole technique, the left pole is thrust forward and planted in the snow as the right foot is pushed forward. Pressure on the left pole at the same time the right foot is advanced will push the right ski into a glide. As the glide slows down, the left foot, with the right pole, repeats the process *(Figure 59)*.

Walking can also be done using both poles simultaneously. This is similar to ice skating. As each foot is alternately placed on the snow, both poles are planted, and with a good push, provide a longer glide than the one-pole method *(Figure 60)*. However, the use of two poles also requires considerably more energy than using one pole.

Another gliding technique uses both poles to force ahead both skis, without a step. This method is often used going downhill, to give the skier a rest. When using this two-pole, feet-together technique, a better glide can be achieved by bending both knees at the

One-Pole Walking

Figure 59

In the one-pole technique, with each step the opposite pole is thrust forward and planted in the snow a comfortable distance ahead. Pressure on the pole at the moment the opposite foot slides forward will start the ski gliding. As the glide slows down, the process is repeated with the other foot and pole.

moment of maximum thrust on the poles. The knee bend momentarily unweights the skis (or lightens the weight on them), permitting a longer glide *(Figure 61)*.

Climbing

There are three ways to climb on skis: 1) straight walking, 2) herringbone, and 3) sidestepping. On very gentle inclines, it is possible to continue walking, in stride, taking smaller steps. This is usually the easiest way to climb, but it doesn't work on steep slopes because the skis slide backwards.

The herringbone gets its name from the tracks it leaves in the snow, which resemble the spine of a fish. When using the herringbone, your body faces uphill, the tips of the skis diverge, and the tails remain close together. Both feet are rotated so the toes point to opposite sides. You then walk uphill, one foot at a time, feeling more like a duck than a skier. The key point in the herringbone is to press the inside edge of the ski firmly into the snow with each step. This will prevent the skis from sliding backwards, downhill. Note that to set the inside edges of the skis the knees must be bent

Figure 60

Two-Pole Walking

In the two-pole technique, both poles are planted with each step. As one foot slides forward, pressure on the two poles starts that ski gliding. The two poles continue to be used with each step. To maintain a good pace, the next step should proceed when the glide from the previous step begins to slow down. Using two poles is faster than using one, but it also requires more energy.

and rolled inward, towards each other *(Figure 1, Figure 62, and Figure 63).*

Sidestepping is the third method of climbing. It is the only method that can be used on steep slopes *(Figure 44 and Figure 64).*

Stopping

All skis follow the same techniques and basic skills for stopping. With cross-country skis, the snowplow is the easiest method to learn and use. It is performed by positioning the skis in the shape of a snowplow. The tails of the skis are pushed apart, while the tips remain together *(Figure 41).* However, this position alone will not slow you down unless the skis are also rolled onto their inside edges. This is done by first flexing (bending) the knees and then rolling them inward, towards each other *(Figure 65).*

Edging is the essential basic skill in stopping, and good edge control is related, in part, to your equip-

Two-Pole Gliding

Figure 61

Pushing on both poles with both feet together permits the arms to do most of the work while the legs rest. This method is often used when gliding downhill. Maximum efficiency can be attained by bending your knees and dropping your seat at the same instant you press on your poles. The seat drop lightens the weight on your feet (unweighting) at the moment of pole thrust, thereby giving you a longer glide.

A

B

Figure 62

Herringbone

The herringbone method of climbing sets the inside edge of each ski *firmly* into the snow so it will hold while taking the next step. The key points in performing the herringbone are: **1)** Keep the feet quite far apart so the tail of the stepping ski can get past the forward leg; **2)** keep the knees bent; **3)** plant each ski on its inside edge firmly so it digs into the snow; and **4)** lean your body forward, up the hill. The poles can be used for balance, but they are not essential for the herringbone.

ment. The stiff boots and fixed-heel bindings of downhill skis allow the skis to respond instantaneously to minute knee movements. In contrast, the flexible boots and free-heel bindings of cross-country skis cause the skis to edge slowly and minimally when the knees roll inward (knee angulation) to set the edges. As a result, the leg actions to edge cross-country skis often must be exaggerated to make the skis respond. Difficulty in stopping is either because you are not getting the tails of your skis far enough apart or because you are failing to roll your knees inward enough to feel a good edgeset. Bent and angulated knees are the key to successful edging, and edging is what controls deceleration and stopping.

Stopping on skis is also possible by turning the skis away from the fall line. On cross-country skis, snowplow and stem turns are the most commonly used. A similar turn, which utilizes the same knee action, is steering. Steering to a stop is a technique for

Herringbone

Figure 63

The herringbone without poles. (Photo by Martin Luray, reprinted from *The Complete Guide to Cross-Country Skiing and Touring* by Martin Luray and Art Tokle, with permission of the authors.)

stopping gradually *(Figure 38)*. These turns are described in the following section.

Another technique for stopping, which can be used in desperation when all else fails, is dragging one or both ski poles through the snow as a brake. This feels a little awkward, but it works *(Figure 66)*!

Turns

Turning on cross-country skis employs the same techniques as on downhill skis. There are two types of turns: two-legged turns, which are parallel turns, and one-legged turns, in which the turn is performed on

Figure 64

Sidestepping

The sidestep is the only method that can be used for slopes too steep for the herringbone. It is easier and requires less vigor than the herringbone. It is also slower. To sidestep, stand sideways to the slope and step upwards. Plant the *outside* edge of the ski firmly in the snow, then bring the lower ski up to the first one. The *inside* edge of the lower ski is dug into the snow to hold your position while you step uphill again. The poles are not needed to side-step, except for balance. They can be pointed behind you to keep them out of the way.

one ski only. (See stem and snowplow turns, Chapter 4.) While the goal of most downhill skiers is to master parallel turns, this is usually not a goal of cross-country skiers. The binding on a cross-country ski holds only the toe of the boot to the ski. The heel is free to move up and down. This makes turning harder to perform than on downhill skis, which fix the whole boot to the ski *(Figure 67).* Parallel turns, which require taking your weight off the skis for a moment (unweighting) and rotating both skis simultaneously, are infrequently performed on cross-country skis because the skis will not unweight and pivot easily, in the same way as downhill skis. Therefore, one-legged turns, which do not require unweighting and pivoting, generally are used for cross-country skiing.

Stem and *snowplow* turns are very similar and

Snowplow Stop

Figure 65

A) In the snowplow, your skis are positioned with their tips together and their heels apart. **B)** Your knees are flexed. The flexed knees do not help you stop. They are only a preparatory action to permit your knees to roll inward. **C)** Rolling your knees toward each other places the skis on their inside edges. It is the bite of the inside edges which lets you slow down and stop. To increase the braking power of the snowplow, keep pushing your heels outward and roll your knees closer together. If your ski tips tend to separate, push your knees forward a bit so there is at least as much weight on your toes as on your heels. (It is when you place more weight on your heels that your ski tips tend to separate.)

A

B

C

Figure 66

Braking with Poles

Braking. Dragging your poles will help to slow you down, particularly when you are heading down a steep slope. (Photo by Martin Luray; reprinted from *The Complete Guide to Cross-Country Skiing and Touring* by Martin Luray and Art Tokle, with permission of the authors.)

employ the same principles. Indeed, the turning portion of the two turns is identical. They differ only in their initiating phase. In a snowplow turn, the skis first assume a snowplow position. This can be used for deceleration. The second step is to shift weight by pushing your *hip* over the turning ski *(Figure 68)*. (To turn right, transfer weight to the left ski.) Maintain your weight on that ski until you have turned as far as you wish. (If you keep your weight there indefinitely, your skis will turn uphill and eventually will stop.) Bring the skis together, parallel to each other, to stop the turn. Or, to turn in the opposite direction, transfer your weight to the other ski, by shifting your hips.

Stem turns are performed in the same way as snowplow turns except there is no preliminary snowplow position. From a parallel position, the tail of just the turning ski is pushed outward in the position of half a snowplow. The hips shift your weight to the turning ski, and the turn proceeds in the same way as a snowplow turn *(Figure 9 and Figure 69)*.

In both stem and snowplow turns, the essential ingredient for a good turn is to roll the turning ski onto its inside edge. Just as mentioned for stopping, positioning a ski on its inside edge requires not only inward knee angulation, but also knee flexion *(Figures 9 and 41)*.

Cross-Country vs. Downhill Binding

Figure 67

The major difference between cross-country and downhill skis is the binding. **A)** The cross-country binding fixes the toe only. The heel is loose and free to lift. This is designed to facilitate walking and gliding, the main actions in this type of skiing. However, the loose heel is a disadvantage for turning and stopping. **B)** The binding of a downhill ski has a fixed heel as well as a fixed toe. The fixed heel gives better control for turns and stops, but makes walking and gliding more difficult.

A

B

Figure 68

Snowplow Turn

From a snowplow position with tips together and tails apart, turns are executed by shifting weight to the ski that is facing in the desired direction. To turn, it is essential that the ski rest on its inside edge. This is done by first flexing the knee, then rolling it inward. The hips shift their weight to the turning ski. **A)** Left turn. The skier first flexes and rolls the right knee inward, then shifts her hips over the right ski. The non-turning left ski has little weight on it and does not participate in the turn. **B)** Right turn. To turn right, the skier flexes and rolls the left knee inward while shifting the hips to the left, so most of her weight is on the left ski. Note that the left ski is sitting on its inside edge, while the right ski (non-turning ski) is almost flat.

A B

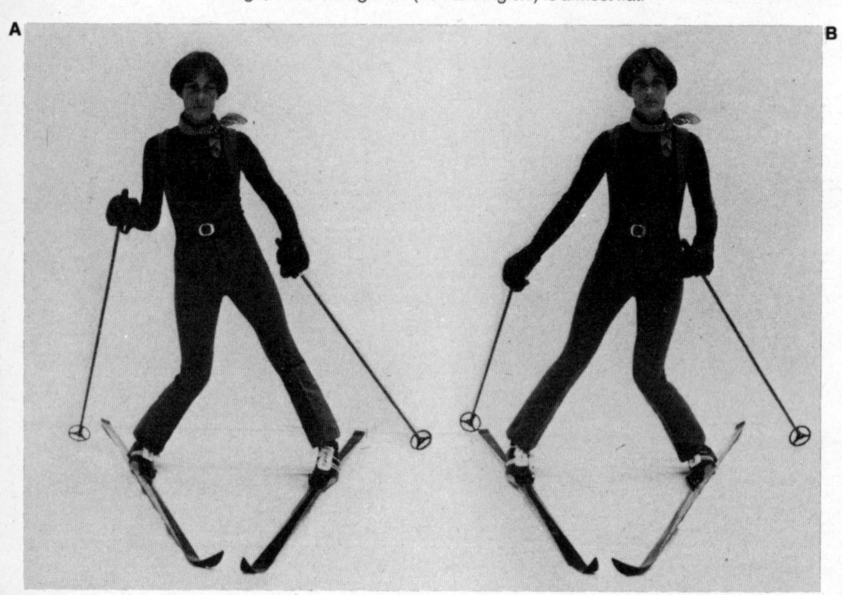

Steering

"Steering" is another method of making a gradual turn on cross-country skis. Steering can be performed from a stem or snowplow position using one leg, or steering can be done with both legs from a parallel position *(Figures 29 and 40)*. The knees of the steering legs are flexed and move sideways in the direction of the turn. While the knees are rolled to the side, the feet also try to pivot the skis in the direction of the turn. The result is a gradual change of direction without unweighting and without transferring weight from one leg to the other.

Telemark

The telemark turn holds a fascination—a mystique—for many Nordic skiers. It is an unusual turn because it is different from any other turn in Nordic or Alpine ski-

Stem Turn

Figure 69

The stem turn follows the same principles as the snowplow turn. The main difference is that it begins with the feet parallel rather than in the wedge position. **A)** The skis are together, prior to the turn. **B)** The heel of the left ski is pushed outward in a half-snowplow position. Note that the knee is flexed and rolled inward. These two actions are the important elements in setting the ski on its inside edge. **C)** The body's weight is shifted by moving the hips sideways, so more weight is shifted to the turning ski. In this case, the skier is turning right by shifting her hips over the left ski, which is already positioned on its inside edge. The weight is held over the turning ski until you wish to stop turning.

A

B

C

ing. The telemark is a modified stem turn performed by positioning the turning ski on its inside edge, just as is done in any stem turn. It is the other ski, the non-turning ski, which makes the telemark so unique. In an ordinary stem turn, the non-turning ski follows along passively, but when doing a telemark, the knee of the non-turning ski is flexed so it rests on the top of the ski. This ski also runs more than a foot behind the turning ski.

This position lowers the body's center of gravity, thereby providing more stability. The lower body position also permits the turning ski to roll further onto its inside edge, producing a little sharper and more controlled turn.

The telemark is possible because of the free-heel binding of the cross-country ski; it is not possible on a downhill ski because the binding fixes the heel to the ski.

The telemark position can also be used for straight running. It is used on rough, bumpy snow by pushing one leg ahead and dropping the knee of the trailing leg onto the top of its ski.

Tips on Learning Turns

1) *Learn on downhill skis.* Because it is easier to turn and to feel edge control on downhill skis, one can learn these skills faster by using a pair of stiff boots and fixed binding.

2) *Learn on short skis.* Because it is easier to control a short ski than a long one, beginners should start with the shorter lengths. Once you've learned to control the edges, graduate to longer lengths, as these are faster and a little more stable.

3) *Learn on packed slopes.* It is more difficult and requires much more energy to turn in deep powder snow than on packed slopes. Since the skills of turning and stopping are the same for all snow conditions, the novice can master them more easily on packed slopes. Once you've developed the techniques on packed snow, they will also be effective in powder.

Turning Around

It is sometimes necessary to change direction from a standing position. This can be done in two ways. The simplest is to pivot the tip of one ski in the new direction, then bring the second ski alongside it. On steep slopes, this can be difficult because it is a slow

Kick Turn

Figures 70A and 70B

The kick turn requires agility and limber legs. **A)** Begin with the skis parallel, facing across the hill. **B)** The downhill ski is kicked up to a vertical position, and **C)** the momentum of the ski moving upwards is continued by twisting the toes away from your body and setting the ski down, now pointing in the opposite direction. **D)** The turn is completed by lifting the remaining ski upwards and pivoting it so it lies parallel to the first ski. In deep snow, it is important to get the heel out of the snow (Figure B) by both kicking high and bending your toes forcefully toward your knee (dorsi-flexion).

A

B

Figures 70C and 70D **C**

D

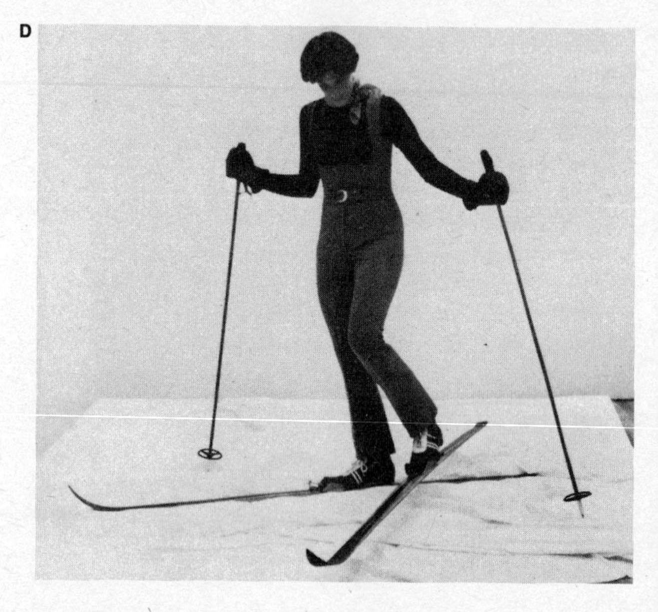

technique and you can start racing downhill as your ski tips cross the fall line.

The other method of changing direction is the kick-turn, which is used in downhill skiing too. One ski, usually the lower one, is kicked forward and quickly turned

180° to face in the opposite direction. The second ski is then lifted out of the snow and brought around to join the first one. One reason the kick-turn is difficult to perform is that many people have trouble turning one foot 180° away from the other *(Figures 70A, 70B, 70C and 70D)*.

Kick-turns should be executed quickly, with decisive, firm steps. With cross-country skis, flex the ankle quickly and deliberately upwards, to get the tail of the ski out of the snow. The loose heel of a cross-country ski makes it more difficult to turn than a downhill ski.

Part IV

Health and Safety on the Slopes

by Richard J. Sanders, M.D., and Barry Lindenbaum, M.D.

24

Conditioning

Consultant: Dr. Phillip S. Wolf

Getting in Shape

Getting your body "in shape" for skiing will make this sport not only more enjoyable but safer. Many injuries occur because a fatigued body and tired legs could not respond quickly enough to conditions on the slope. Ideally, one should keep in shape year round by participating in physical activities or a program of regular exercise. However, because a few of the muscles used in skiing are seldom used in other sports, even those people who stay in good physical condition year-round may need specific muscle exercises to prepare for skiing.

Conditioning for skiing has two goals: to develop the heart and lungs to deliver the largest possible amount of oxygen to the muscles, and to train the leg muscles used in skiing to more effectively use this oxygen for greater strength and endurance.

Each individual has his/her own maximum potential for heart, lung, and muscle performance, which can only be reached through training.

Heart and Lung Conditioning

"Training" for skiing includes everything from preparing for a weekend of easy fun on the slopes to conditioning for a season of downhill racing. Define your goals from the start, because even though the principles of conditioning remain the same at all levels, the time and effort devoted to getting into shape will depend upon the type of skiing you plan to do.

The average adult recreational skier who wishes to prepare for several full days of moderate to vigorous skiing requires some pre-season heart and lung

Maximum Achievable Pulse Rate

The pulse rate is the number of times the heart beats each minute. The maximum pulse rate is the fastest rate attainable for a given heart. The heart of a youngster can perform at rates greater than 200 beats a minute, but with increasing years, the peak performance rate of the heart is reduced. "Conditioning" the heart—that is, training the heart muscle to perform more work with each heartbeat—occurs best when the pulse rate is maintained at levels between 70 and 85 percent of the maximum pulse rate. This table shows how the maximum achievable pulse rate reduces with age.

Age	Maximum* pulse rate	85 percent of maximum	70 percent of maximum
25	200	170	140
30	194	165	136
35	188	160	132
40	182	155	128
45	176	150	124
50	171	145	119
55	165	140	115
60	159	135	111
65	153	130	107
70	147	125	103

*Beats per minute

conditioning to build endurance. There are several exercises for heart and lung conditioning. Running and jogging are the most common ones, but swimming, cycling, handball, tennis, squash, basketball, and several others serve the same purpose. The accepted guideline for the degree of stress an exercise exerts on the heart and lungs is the heart rate (pulse beat). In general, the faster the pulse the greater the stress, and the greater will be its beneficial conditioning effect.

Knowing how to measure your pulse is helpful in conditioning. The easiest place to feel it is in your neck, alongside your windpipe *(Figure 71A)*. Or you can try your wrist, just above your thumb *(Figure 71B)*. Use a watch with a second hand, count the number of pulse beats in 6 seconds, and multiply this by 10.

The goal for a moderate training response is to exercise vigorously enough to increase your pulse rate to at least 70 percent of maximum (see the table above) and maintain it there for 20 minutes or more three times a week. More conditioning can be obtained by pushing

Taking Your Pulse

Figure 71

Two easy spots to count your pulse are **A)** the side of your neck and **B)** your wrist.

A

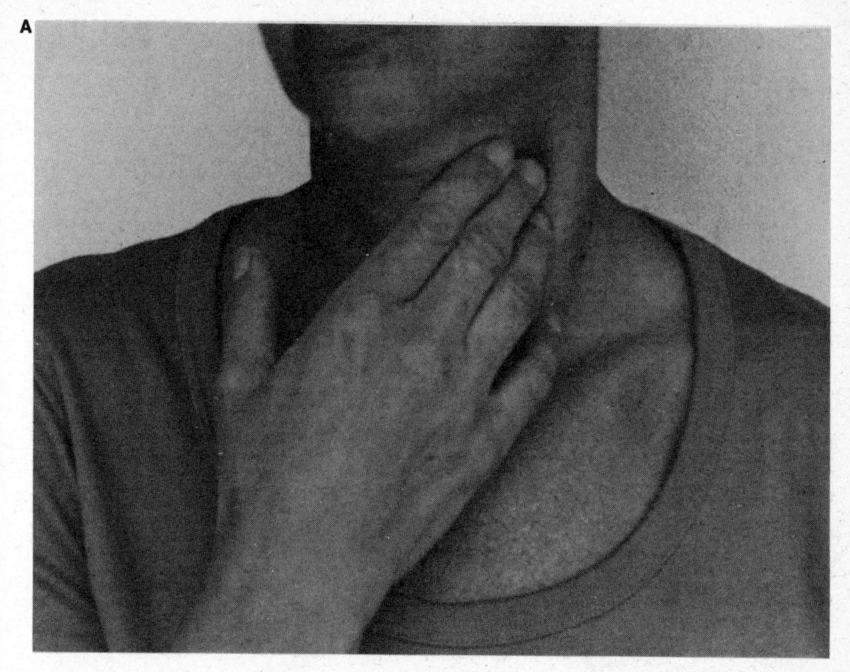

B

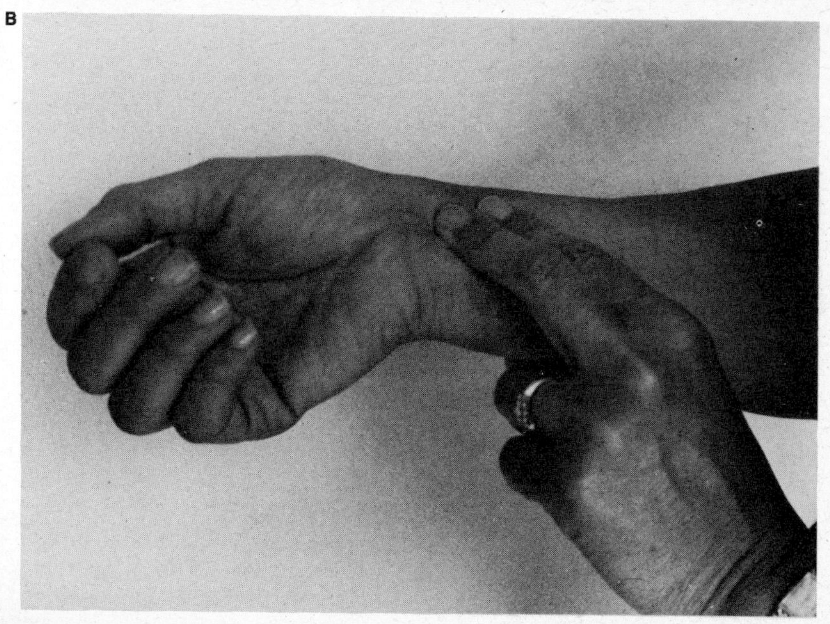

Figure 72

Muscle-Strengthening Exercises

The major muscle groups used in skiing can be stretched and strengthened by holding this position for several minutes a day; it is the basic skiing position. Dropping your seat over your heels results in flexion of the ankle and knee joints, as well as the waist. This exercise can be performed while doing other activities, such as talking on the telephone, washing your hands and face, combing or drying your hair, brushing your teeth, or shaving. Once in this position, spend a portion of the time with your knees facing forward as well as rolled to one side and then the other side.

A

your pulse rate to 85 percent of maximum. The maximum achievable pulse rate varies with age. While twenty-year-olds have a maximum level near 200 beats per minute, seventy-year-olds have a maximum rate closer to 150.

When starting an exercise program, establish a training goal. Decide the pulse rate you wish to reach, how long you'd like to maintain it, and the number of times a week you can exercise. In setting this goal, keep in mind the age limitations on maximum pulse rate. If you have heart or lung disease you should not undertake a strenuous program without consulting your physician. Allow 6 to 12 weeks of gradually building up the amount of exercise you perform until you reach your goal. Some excellent books that provide

B

C

Figure 73

Variations in Muscle-Strengthening Exercises

Variations in muscle-strengthening exercises are achieved by increasing the length of time each position is held. When starting, two minutes may be all you can hold. With daily practice, exceeding five minutes should be your goal. When you can hold a position for over five minutes, increase the degree of knee flexion, as shown from A to B. To maintain balance as your knee flexion approaches 90°, it will be necessary to flex forward at the waist. To further stress and strengthen the thigh muscles, your weight can be transferred backwards, from the center of your feet towards your heels, as shown in C. Take this step when you can hold the position in B for over five minutes.

A

helpful details on these conditioning programs are *The Complete Book of Running* by James F. Fixx and *The New Aerobics* by Kenneth Cooper.

Specific Muscle Training

While skiing uses many of the body's muscles, certain thigh muscles are utilized far more than others. These muscles are not as important in other sports, nor are they adequately conditioned by running, cycling, swimming, or other common exercises. For this reason, skiing itself is the best way to train for skiing because it will build up the appropriate muscles in the required way. However, for most skiers this is not possible in the off-season. These skiers should exercise the specific muscle groups used most in skiing in

B

C

other ways. These groups are the quadriceps femoris (the extensors), the hamstrings (flexors), the adductors, and the buttock muscles (rotators). Many exercises are recommended for strengthening and training these muscles, including deep knee bends, wall sitting, pressing weights, jumping rope or benches. Each exercise conditions at least one muscle group. However, specific muscle conditioning requires a regular exercise schedule (as described in *Ski Conditioning* by M. L. Foss and J. G. Garrick, John Wiley & Sons, N.Y., 1978).

Many skiers find it difficult to exercise on a regular basis. The best way for them to train the specific muscle groups used in skiing is to stand in the knee-flexed skiing position for several minutes a day. This exercise stretches and strengthens all of the thigh and leg muscles used in skiing. The knee-flexed position is the most strenuous position employed in skiing, and practicing it ahead of time will improve your skiing ability in general as well as strengthen the thigh muscles.

An advantage of this static exercise is that it can be done while doing other things, so that you need not reserve daily exercise time. During the course of each day take five to ten minutes to stand still and perform this simple conditioning exercise. It can be done while talking on the telephone, washing your hands and face, combing or drying your hair, brushing your teeth, or shaving.

Begin by dropping your seat over your heels, thus flexing both knees and ankles. In the correct position you should feel some weight on your heels and some on your toes. You should feel comfortably balanced and not as though you are teetering forward and backward. Once you're in the knee-flexed position, your knees can be rolled from one side to the other or kept straight ahead *(Figures 72A, 72B, and 72C)*.

The two variables in this exercise are length of time and degree of flexion. In general, greater degrees of flexion held for longer periods of time will provide more conditioning for the thigh and leg muscles. Start with a degree of flexion that you can hold for at least two minutes. When you can maintain it for five minutes, increase the degree of flexion. Vigorous and deep-powder skiers should aim for a goal of close to 90° flexion held for at least five minutes *(Figures 73A, 73B and*

73C). For the best effects, begin exercising at least a couple of months before the ski season and continue through the winter. Since this type of conditioning requires no extra time in your daily routine, it can easily be continued year-round, which is the ideal way to keep these muscles in shape. Using a stop watch to time yourself is very helpful.

The exercises just described put significant stress on the surfaces of the knee joints. As a result, they can be painful to people who have inflammation or arthritis in their knees (a condition called chondromalacia). If you already have pain, swelling, or joint instability in your knees, or if pain develops in the joints after starting these exercises, you should consult a physician before continuing them. There are alternative methods for strengthening the thigh muscles, which include isometric straight-leg raising and short-arc quadriceps-strengthening exercises. Instructions for these should be individualized and can be obtained from a physician or physical therapist.

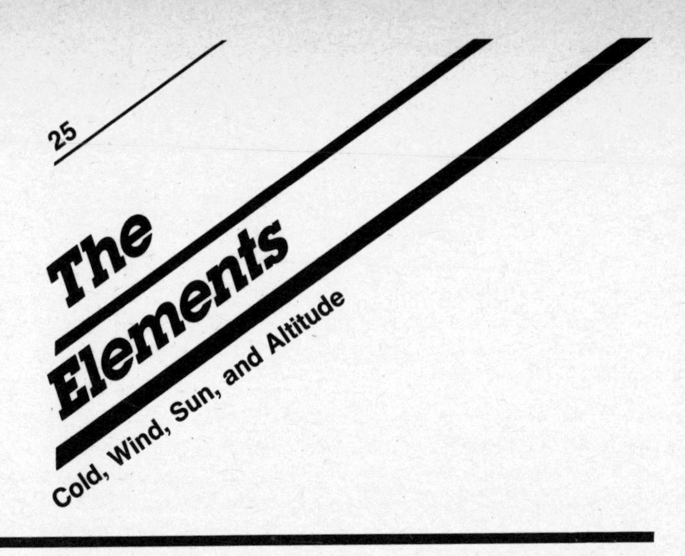

Frostbite

Frostbite occurs from inadequate skin protection during exposure to cold temperatures. It develops first on those parts of the body that are isolated from the body's central core: the fingers, toes, ears, and nose. As it progresses, frostbite reaches the hands, feet, and face. Prolonged exposure to cold lowers the temperature of the central core, produces unconsciousness, and eventually can lead to death.

To prevent frostbite, begin by keeping the trunk warm. Inadequate protection of the torso causes diminished blood supply to the hands and feet, which is the body's way of preserving heat for the vital organs. Therefore, warm sweaters, jackets, and vests are important on cold days to provide maximum warmth to the extremities.

In freezing weather, insulated gloves or mittens are essential. Down is an excellent insulator, but loses most of its effectiveness when wet. Other natural and synthetic fibers are as warm as down and are more reliable when wet. Mittens are warmer than gloves because the heat from each finger keeps adjacent fingers warm. In addition, mittens have less surface area exposed to the cold than gloves. Moisture makes an insulator less effective. A good waterproof, or at least water-resistant, covering is very important for gloves and mittens. Once they become wet, the cold temperature is transmitted through the moisture to the skin.

Boots, like gloves, should be insulated and water resistant. While the shells of plastic boots are completely waterproof, snow can work its way into the crevices between each half of the shell, and then to the interior of the boots. Keeping the lowest boot buckle closed helps the boots remain dry. However, the boots should not be tight against the toes. While tight boots make the ski respond more quickly to foot movements, the tightness should be limited to the ankle and heel. Air space for the toes insulates the feet.

Whenever the hands and feet become so cold that numbness or pain develops in the fingers or toes, it is essential to warm up. Numbness, tingling, and pain are the feelings experienced when the life of a finger or toe is threatened. Rarely will permanent damage result if these sensations are present for less than 30 minutes. However, if they persist for several hours, first the skin and then the deeper structures can be damaged. Sometimes the body will be able to recover, but at other times permanent disabilities ensue. Amputation of fingers, toes, or even more can result from simple frostbite.

The exposed parts of the face, particularly the lobes of the ears, the tip of the nose, and the cheeks, are the next most likely parts to suffer frostbite. Strong winds on cold days can produce temperatures as low as 60° below zero, even in bright sunshine. Frostbite on the face can develop in just a few minutes under these conditions. Often, the whole body feels so cold that you are unaware of frostbite developing on your face. At such times, skiing with a partner is important. The first sign of frostbite is a white color developing in areas that normally are pink. In very cold environments, partners should look at each other's faces and inform each other of white spots. Blowing exhaled air against a glove held immediately in front of the mouth will usually provide enough warmth to restore circulation to the exposed face. A hat or wool band pulled over the ear lobes so they are covered completely should protect the ears. A face mask protects the nose, lips, and chin.

Rapid warming is the treatment for frostbite that has reached the state of pain or numbness. Rubbing with snow or ice will make matters worse. The sooner the part is warmed, the less the possible damage. Warm water is better than warm air. Water at a temperature of

104–107° Fahrenheit (40–42° centigrade) is ideal. If a thermometer is not available, use water that feels warm to the hand, but not hot. Once the part has been warmed, nothing more can be done. Only time will determine if permanent damage has occurred.

If frostbite occurs in a situation where the victim must walk some distance to reach an adequate shelter, rewarming should be delayed until the shelter is reached. It will only be possible to walk on an injured leg, for example, while it is cold. Once the leg has been rewarmed, the pain will be too severe for walking.

Hypothermia

While frostbite refers to injuring the extremities and other areas of skin by exposure to cold temperatures, hypothermia (meaning subnormal body temperature) is the term used to describe the effect on the whole body of freezing temperatures. This is rarely seen in patrolled ski areas because it takes many hours of exposure to cold to even begin to lower the body's temperature. However, should a person become stranded overnight in the cold without adequate protection, hypothermia can occur and can be fatal.

Preserving the body's heat is primarily a matter of wearing the proper type of clothing. Clothes that are heaviest in weight are not necessarily the best insulators. Here are a few guidelines to adequate warmth when skiing:

—Several thin layers of clothing can be more effective than a single heavy layer. The air trapped between the clothing layers provides good insulation.

—A cotton layer against the skin absorbs moisture from sweating. It acts as a wick carrying moisture away from the skin.

—Wool holds heat better than cotton, and wool retains heat better than other materials when wet.

—Nylon will absorb very little moisture and is an excellent wind shield.

—A good combination of clothing consists of a cotton layer against the skin, a wool layer over the cotton, and an outer covering of nylon or similar water-repellent fabric. Additional layers of insulation, such as down- or fiber-filled jackets, provide extra and needed protection in colder weather.

—High-waisted pants, bibs, or one-piece suits keep snow and cold from entering at the waistline. These garments offer more warmth than conventional ski pants.

—Even on warm, sunny days, carry extra clothing with you. Mountain weather can change quickly and dramatically.

The signs of hypothermia are shivering, a rapid pulse, fast breathing, and pale skin color. As the condition worsens, the victim stops shivering, becomes confused and eventually loses consciousness.

The treatment of hypothermia is rapid rewarming. A tub of hot water at a temperature of 104–112° Fahrenheit (40–44° centigrade) is ideal. If a thermometer is not available, use water that feels warm to your hand, but not so hot that it is uncomfortable. If a tub is not available, use hot-water bottles and warm blankets to keep the victim in as warm an environment as possible. Direct the rewarming to the torso, not to the extremities, because obviously it is critical to survival to keep the vital organs warm and functioning.

Wind

The wind is seldom regarded as a significant element of danger, except when it is violent and reaches storm levels. However, even mild winds alter the effective outside temperature. For example, if you are riding a chair lift on a sunny afternoon when the thermometer reads 30°F and there is a moderate wind of 15 mph, the effective temperature on your face is only 9°F (see the wind-chill chart on page 154). The wind-chill factor is the lowering of effective atmospheric temperatures by the wind. In general, for each mile per hour of wind, the effective outdoor temperature is lowered 1–2° Fahrenheit. Beyond 40 mph, there is very little additional chilling effect. The wind has a relatively greater cooling effect at lower temperature than at higher ones. A 20 mph wind will lower an atmospheric temperature of 40°F to 18°F, a decrease of 22°F. But the same 20 mph wind will lower the effective temperature of 56°F below zero to 96°F below zero, a fall of 40°F.

Wind increases the risk of frostbite and hypothermia. The risk of damage increases greatly at effective temperatures under 20°F below zero. Above this level proper clothing will usually give adequate protection, while below this temperature prolonged exposure can cause frostbite despite good clothing.

Wind also tends to dry the skin if the body's natural

Wind-Chill Chart

Wind reduces the effective atmospheric temperature. Warm temperatures are lowered approximately 1°F for each mile per hour of wind. Colder temperatures, below zero degrees F, are further reduced—up to 2° F for each mile per hour of wind. Winds of over 40 miles per hour elicit the same reduction as winds of 40 miles per hour.

Wind mph	**Effective Temperature in Degrees Fahrenheit**								
0	40°	30°	20°	10°	0°	−10°	−20°	−30°	−40°
5	37	28	16	6	− 5	−15	−26	−36	−47
10	28	16	4	−9	−21	−33	−46	−58	−70
15	22	9	−5	−18	−36	−45	−58	−72	−85
20	18	4	−10	−25	−39	−53	−67	−82	−96
25	16	0	−15	−29	−44	−59	−74	−83	−104
30	13	−2	−18	−33	−48	−63	−79	−94	−109
35	11	−4	−20	−35	−49	−64	−82	−98	−113
40	10	−6	−21	−37	−53	−69	−85	−102	−116

oil is not supplemented. Commercially available skin lotions should be used whenever there is prolonged exposure to the elements.

Sunburn

When you are enjoying a bright sunny day on the slopes, it is wise to bear in mind the discomfort that can result from overexposure of the skin to the sun's ultraviolet rays. These rays are filtered by the atmosphere above the earth. The thinner the atmosphere, the more intense are the ultraviolet rays that penetrate it. This explains why you are more apt to get severe sunburns at midday and at high altitudes. At midday, the sun has less atmosphere to penetrate than early or late in the day when the sun is at small angles to the horizon and must go through much more atmosphere to reach you. Also, at high altitudes, there is less atmosphere to filter the sun's rays than at sea level. If you ski at Vail or Aspen, where the altitude at the base is greater than 7,000 feet, there is 20 to 25 percent less atmospheric air to block the sun's ultraviolet rays.

Clouds act as excellent filters. However, the protection afforded by clouds depends on how thick and heavy they are; light, high clouds may not filter out all of the ultraviolet rays. You should beware of the potential of getting a severe sunburn on a cloudy day, if the clouds are thin.

As springtime approaches, the earth moves closer to the sun than in winter, thereby increasing the intensity of the sun's rays. This is one of the reasons severe sunburns are more common near the end of the ski season.

Your body has some built-in protection from the sun in its pigmentation. If you have very dark skin, you probably don't have to worry about a sunburn. If your skin is fair, you should protect yourself in the sun. A thin layer of clothing is adequate protection for most of your body. However, the exposed areas of your face require some ointment or lotion to either absorb or reflect the sun's ultraviolet rays. Be sure also to apply the sun protector to the sheltered areas of your face—under the chin, nose, and upper lip. These areas receive ultraviolet rays that are reflected upwards from the snow on the ground.

Photosensitivity

If you take medication for *any* reason, you should be aware that certain drugs can increase the sensitivity of your skin to the sun. The skin's reaction may be either an excessive sunburn or a skin rash. Some of the drugs which are known to cause light photosensitivity are: tetracyclines, sulfonamides, sulfonylureas, chlorothiazides, hologenated salicylanilides, phenothiazides, and furocoumarins.

The Eyes

Consultant: Dr. Harold Leight

Bright sun shining on open snow fields is more dangerous to your eyes than bright sun in other places. The crystals reflect ultraviolet rays from the snow's surface upwards, towards the eyes. As a result, your eyes are exposed to the sun's rays even though you are not looking directly toward the sun. The commonest injury is an ultraviolet burn of the cornea or the conjunctiva, the outer covering of the white part of the eye. The damage can occur without warning or pain. Ultraviolet burns of the cornea damage only the outer layers of the cornea. Healing usually occurs within several days, without permanent damage. However, corneal burns are very painful, and to relieve the pain it is often necessary to keep the eyes closed for a few days by using an eye patch.

Glasses or goggles large enough to cover both eyes entirely will prevent eye damage. Contact lenses will protect the cornea, the most painful area when burned, but not the conjunctiva. Because ultraviolet rays are stopped by any type and any color of glasses, the quality and color of the glasses is not important. The cheapest pair will suffice.

Long-wave (infrared) damage to the eye is rarely seen in skiers. It is caused by looking directly at the sun, without protection, for a long period of time.

"Snow blindness" is a term meaning dimness of vision due to the glare of the sun upon the snow. It does not necessarily imply eye damage. It occurs when normal eyes are suddenly exposed to bright sunlight. This is relieved immediately by wearing dark glasses. However, snow blindness also occurs when the cornea has been sunburned, which may require a few days to improve.

High-Altitude Sickness

Consultant: Dr. Albert Guggenheim

At high altitudes the air contains less oxygen than at sea level. The body accommodates itself to this thinner air by adjusting its breathing and circulatory systems. However, these changes do not occur instantaneously. Adaptation often requires at least a day or two and sometimes much longer. People accustomed to living at sea level who ascend to high altitudes may experience mild or, on occasion, serious discomfort as a result of the quick diminution of oxygen.

Skiers should be aware of two other important conditions that can occur at high altitudes: acute mountain sickness and pulmonary edema. Another condition, seen more often in mountain climbers than skiers, is acute cerebral edema.

■ *Acute mountain sickness.* Acute mountain sickness is caused by the combination of decreased oxygen in the air and strenuous physical exercise, which requires increased oxygen. In some people, just the altitude change results in this discomfort. Shortness of breath, blue lips and fingernails, headache, dizziness, fatigue, and disburbances in vision are the common symptoms.

Skiers who have had acute mountain sickness in the past may be able to prevent or ameliorate the condition in the future. They should come to the ski area a couple of days early or take it easy for the first day or two on the slopes.

Treatment for acute mountain sickness is oxygen and rest. If the symptoms are severe, or do not improve in a short time, suspect the more serious condition, pulmonary edema, and seek medical consultation.

■ *Pulmonary edema.* Pulmonary edema (fluid in the lungs) is a dangerous condition caused by lack of oxygen. High-altitude pulmonary edema develops when a person ascends from sea level to higher elevations, usually over 9,000 feet.

Pulmonary edema will generally become evident within a few hours to a couple of days of the time of arrival at the higher elevation. The symptoms include severe shortness of breath, an annoying dry cough, tightness in the chest, headache, weakness, palpitation of the heart, and bloody sputum.

Treatment of pulmonary edema is immediate return to a lower altitude, rest, and oxygen. A physician should be consulted. At times it may be difficult to differentiate acute mountain sickness from pulmonary edema. In such cases, medical attention must be obtained. If the shortness of breath persists for more than a few hours, the skier should be regarded as having the more serious condition and moved to a lower altitude.

■ *Acute cerebral edema.* Cerebral edema means fluid or swelling in the brain. It occasionally occurs at high altitudes for reasons that are not understood. Because it is a serious condition, it is important to know how to recognize it. The signs of high-altitude brain swelling are severe headaches, hallucinations, staggered walking, double vision, emotional instability, disorientation, confusion, and at times, projectile vomiting. It can progress to unconsciousness and death.

The treatment of acute high-altitude cerebral edema is immediate descent to a lower altitude. Two drugs given intravenously may also be helpful if available: 1) cortisone compounds—dexamethasone, betamethasone, or others; 2) diuretics—furosemide (Lasix), nitol, or others.

26

Slope Safety

Equipment

Bindings

Safety bindings are the single most important safety feature in skiing. Failure of these bindings to release is the major cause of most lower-extremity injuries. While there are a variety of different bindings manufactured today, all are based on the principle that when enough stress or force is exerted on the leg, the binding will release *before* an injury occurs.

Leg injuries—damaged ligaments, muscles, joints, or fractured bones—usually happen when the ski and the upper body are moving in different directions or at different speeds. The leg is caught between these two opposing forces, and if the forces cannot be resolved (by the release of the ski from the leg), something in the leg will tear or break.

The safety binding can be regarded, in principle, as a spring fixing the boot to the ski. When the spring is twisted or pulled with enough force, it will release the attachment between boot and ski. By increasing the tension on the spring, more force will be required before the binding releases. Similarly, reducing the tension of the spring will let it release under less stress. To work effectively, all parts of a safety binding must be operating properly. Below are some guidelines to observe in order to derive maximum protection from your safety bindings.

1) Rust, ice, or dirt can prevent proper binding release. Bindings should be checked each season, lubricated when necessary, and replaced if the release mechanism is not smooth. The release mechanism should be checked each time the skis are put on, because ice can form in a binding while the skis are outside at lunchtime, or dirt can collect in the bindings of skis riding exposed on car roofs.

2) Proper tension on the spring is vital to correct operation of the binding. The force required to fracture a leg depends upon the skier's body weight, age, and bone thickness. These can be measured and the binding set to release at a smaller force than is required to break the bones. If you adjust the springs to lower tensions, an even greater safety factor is achieved. However, when the binding is set too loosely, the ski will release when even minor tension is exerted on the binding, and a ski that releases too easily can also cause injuries. Bindings with anti-shock devices are available to absorb these minor stresses which occur when turning at high speeds and in mogul fields. Thus, there is an accepted recommended binding tension for each skier, depending on body build and skiing ability.

As a skier, you should know how to readjust your bindings so they can be altered while skiing. If the skis release when they shouldn't, tighten the bindings gradually. If the skis do not release when you feel they should have, loosen the bindings a little at a time. As a rule, *play safe.* Begin with your bindings on the loose side and tighten them as needed.

3) Many bindings release when the boot moves sideways off the ski. This lateral movement assumes that the bottom of the boot will slide freely over the surface of the ski, with minimal friction or resistance. To assist this free movement, antifriction devices, often made of Teflon, are fixed to the top of the ski *(Figure 74).* It is estimated that these plates can reduce the frictional forces by 70 percent. However, snow or ice that adheres to the bottom of the boot can reduce or eliminate the safety features of the antifriction device. Therefore, it is important to clean the bottom of your boot each time you step into your binding. A small plastic windshield scraper, which will fit in your pocket, can be very helpful.

Safety Straps

Safety straps were designed to be a part of safety bindings. They prevent a released ski from getting lost as well as from running downhill and injuring other skiers. The commonly used safety strap has one end attached

Antifriction Plates

Figure 74

The sole of the boot rests on a smooth antifriction surface, often made of Teflon. When the binding releases, the toe is free to move sideways, and continues to move out of the ski if there is no friction to hold it there. It is important to clean the top of the plate and the bottom of the ski boot each time you step into your skis. Accumulations of snow and ice between the boot and the antifriction plate eliminate the value of this safety device.

to the ski and the other end wrapped around the skier's ankle *(Figure 75A)*. This type of strap has a major disadvantage: The released ski is free to pivot in all directions around the foot, and can hit the skier in the face or elsewhere. While injuries from a free-pivoting ski are infrequent, they do occur.

A safer type of safety strap is the "Arlberg" strap, which is wrapped at least one and a half times around the ankle *(Figure 75B)*. This prevents the released ski from pivoting freely, but still provides the other safety features. The main reason it is not commonly used is that it requires a little more time to fasten and unfasten the buckle.

Ski-brakes (or ski-stops) are another device designed to prevent a released ski from running downhill *(Figure 75C)*. They have the advantage of being unattached to the leg so that when the ski releases, it stays behind. There is little danger of injury by the released ski. The disadvantage of the ski-brake is that the ski

Figure 75

Safety Straps and Brakes

A) The commonly used safety strap, which wraps once around the ankle and is fixed to the binding, prevents the ski from running away when the safety binding releases. However, after it is released, the ski can rotate around the foot and strike the skier in the head or body. **B)** The "Arlberg" strap wraps twice around the ankle. When the ski releases, it is less likely to rotate freely and injure the wearer. In this example, the ends of the straps are fixed to the heel binding. It is still possible for the ski to pivot around the straps, although less likely than in A. A better position for the Arlberg straps is fastened to metal rings mounted on each side of the ski, in the middle of the boot. **C)** The ski brake is a piece of metal attached to a spring which is held under the ski boot. When the boot releases from the ski binding, the brake unsprings into the position shown here. The pointed metal tip digs into the snow, preventing the ski from running freely downhill. The ski is completely detached from the skier. This is probably the safest type of safety strap because the ski cannot pivot around the foot and hit the skier. Its two disadvantages are that the ski can get lost in powder and that the ski will stay at the point of release, while its owner can slide many yards down the hill. It can then be a long walk back uphill to find and retrieve the released ski.

A

can be lost if it releases in deep powder. In addition, if you roll downhill after falling, you may have to climb back uphill to get your ski.

Poles

The conventional ski pole has a wrist strap that is intended to prevent losing the pole *(Figure 76B).* The strap can also be used for extra leverage when poling

B

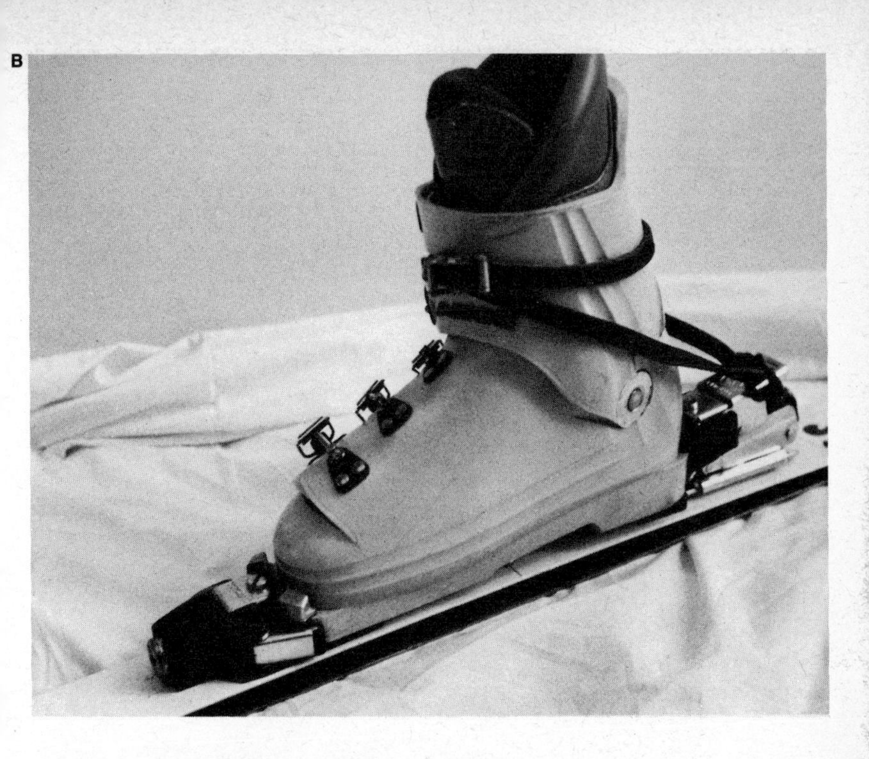

C

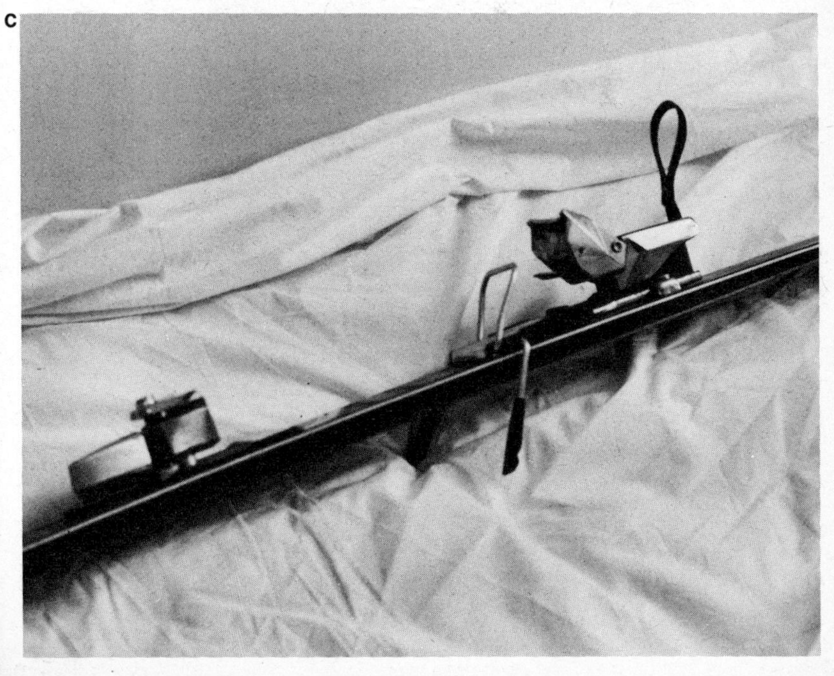

Figure 76

Pole Strap Positions

A) The pole strap is over the whole hand and wrapped under the thumb for extra poling leverage. This can be unsafe if you fall over your pole.
B) The strap is also over the whole hand. This is unsafe in the same way as position A.
C) The strap lies over just four fingers and not the thumb. This is safer than A and B because the pole has a better chance of being released from your hand if you fall.
D) The strap is free, not over the hand or wrist. This is the safest position because you cannot twist your hand, thumb, or shoulder on your pole. If you fall, or the pole becomes caught on a twig, the pole will automatically detach itself from your body.
E) This safety pole has a partial strap over the hand. In a fall, the hand easily pulls out of the partial handle so the arm and shoulder cannot be twisted around the pole. Many people use the pole strap for extra leverage when pole-planting, holding it as in A. However, the same stability and leverage can be found by using a pole with a wide flange under the fifth finger. This is much safer than using the strap around the hand and wrist.

A

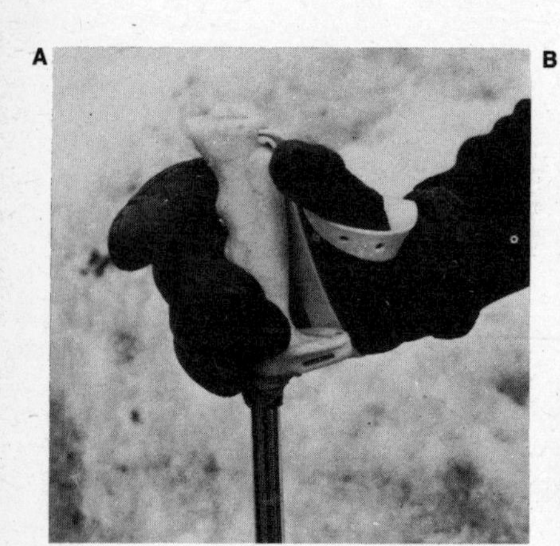

B

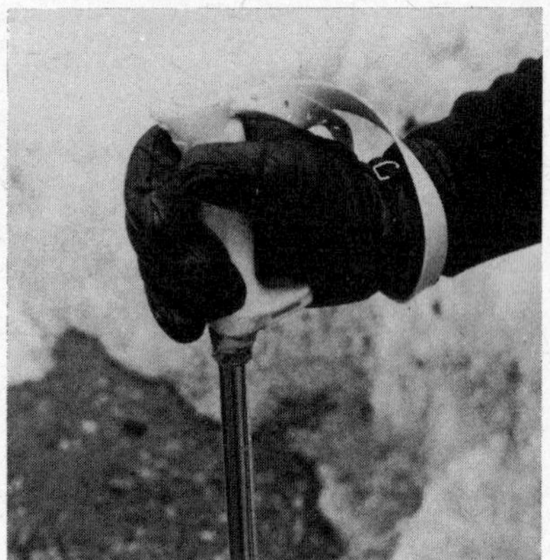

by looping it between the thumb and index finger *(Figure 76A)*. However, this strap can become a distinct liability. If you fall with your pole trapped beneath you, it is possible for the pole to exert enough force on your shoulder, wrist, or thumb to tear some ligaments or cause a dislocation. When you are skiing among obstacles such as trees, the pole basket can catch on roots or fallen branches and result in similar injuries.

To avoid injuries from poles, you should not place the straps over the wrist. They can be looped over the fingers *(Figure 76C)*, omitting the thumb, or even safer, they can be held by the grips alone, without the straps *(Figure 76D)*.

There are a variety of safety poles available. Some of these have straps which release when the pole is caught. Others are constructed with a stiff, partial strap

C

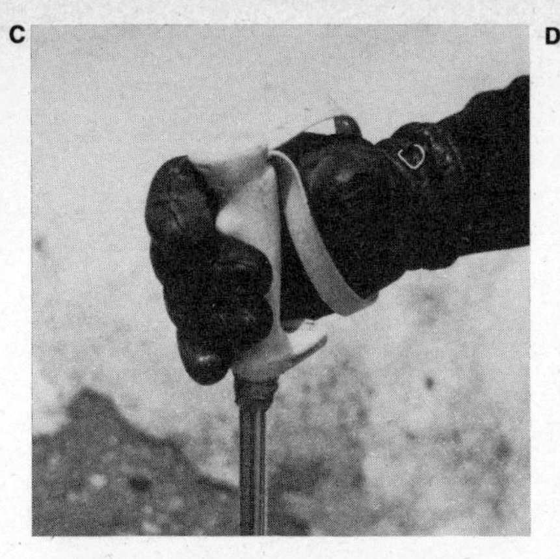

D

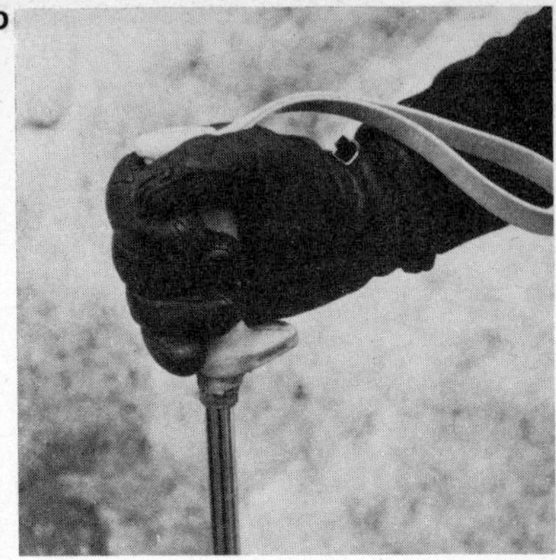

E

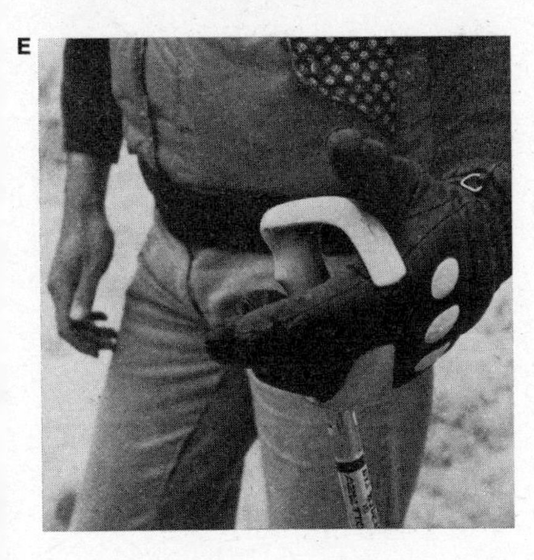

from which the hand can easily escape if the pole is stuck *(Figure 76E).*

The leverage lost by not using the pole strap can be recovered by using a pole grip with a wide flange on its outer side. Such a flange is built into the safety grip shown in Figure 76E and is also a part of the grip illustrated in the other figures.

Glasses and Goggles

Glasses or goggles are important to protect the eyes from the ultraviolet rays of the sun. On snowy days, eye protection is also important to permit visibility. In heavy snowstorms, glasses alone are often inadequate because snow gets on the inside of the glass. On such occasions, goggles are the only solution. They enclose the air space around the glass and prevent snow from entering. The disadvantage of goggles is that heat and moisture from the face can be trapped inside, causing fogging.

Ski goggles are designed for automatic defogging by allowing outside air to flow across the inside of the lens. Goggles should have large enough air vents to permit a rapid air flow and at the same time keep out the snow. Several goggles that are now manufactured offer these features. Even so, all goggles seem to fog when the skier is standing still because very little air flows through. This fogging usually clears up when you start to ski and establish air flow. Goggles are also available with battery-operated motors or heating coils to rapidly defog the inner surface. These are excellent features.

Chemical coating of the surface of the lens can also prevent fogging. Many goggles are coated when they are manufactured, but the coating can wear off. Liquid, plastic, and silicone preparations are available to carry in your pocket to use as needed. Oftentimes, the goggles work well until they get wet inside, following a fall. Then they start to fog. When this happens, it is best to take a minute to dry the inside of the goggles completely and apply a chemical antifog.

The lens color of glasses and goggles is unimportant. Dark glasses provide no more protection from the sun's ultraviolet rays than yellow or plain glasses. The only reason for selecting dark glasses is for personal comfort in reducing the intensity of the sun on very bright days. For the skier who wishes to carry only one lens, yellow is probably the most versatile choice.

Helmets

Concussions, skull fractures, and brain damage can occur from head injuries while skiing. As a rule, serious head injuries only happen to racers going at fast speeds. Helmets should always be worn when racing, but they are usually not necessary at slow speeds.

Rules for the Slope

Courtesy and common sense go a long way towards avoiding ski injuries. Years ago, sailors developed the rules of the "right of way" for sailboats. Their purpose was to insure safe passage for everyone by establishing safety guidelines for all to follow. Traffic lights and stop signs serve the same purpose on streets and highways. Skiing is still a relatively young sport, and skiers have not yet established rigid laws to protect people on the slopes. However, many ski areas post local rules to prevent accidents. Below are a few examples.

1) When one skier is passing another, the skier being passed has the right of way.

2) Stop below, rather than above, your companions. There is less risk of skidding into them.

3) Rest on the side of the slope, not the middle.

4) When entering a new trail, or when starting to ski from the middle of a slope, look uphill and yield to approaching skiers.

5) Do not ski alone on seldom-skied trails.

Defensive Skiing

On roads and highways, defensive driving prevents accidents. This means anticipating the other drivers, being ready to stop if the car ahead of you stops, and having good brakes. Defensive skiing is similar. It means anticipating the actions of the other skiers on the hill, being prepared and able to stop at any time should a hazard appear, and having good "brakes."

Your brakes are the edges of the skis. Not only should the eges be kept sharp, but you must know how to use them. Edging, or effective edge control, is the first, and most important, skill in skiing. The best way to avoid ski injuries is to concentrate on controlling your edges so you will never ski out of control.

Bad weather and icy conditions are as hazardous on the slopes as on the highways. In these conditions, reduced speed is as important in skiing as it is in driving. Just as defensive driving improves your chances of remaining uninjured on the road, defensive skiing will reduce your risks on the slopes.

Tree Skiing

When you are skiing on a wooded slope, two safety features should be observed. First, do not wear ski-pole straps. If a ski pole gets caught on a twig or branch, a pole strap that is looped over the wrist can cause a dislocation or fracture of a shoulder, arm, wrist, or thumb. To prevent this, hold the ski poles by their grips alone, without using the straps, so that if a pole does get caught, it can easily be released. It will be much easier to walk back uphill to recover the pole if you have two good arms to assist the climb.

The second safety feature in trees is eye protection. Small branches hanging a few feet above a trail may not be seen until they have brushed against your face, and possibly your eyes. Goggles or glasses offer continuous protection and should always be worn in wooded areas.

Chair-lift Aids

There are two basic types of chair lifts: those with a center post and those with outside supports. Aside from the position of the supporting poles, the lifts are essentially the same. Getting on and off chair lifts is one of the common causes of injuries, particularly to novice skiers. Here are a few tips.

1) When loading, *think ahead.* Observe the people in front of you. Be mentally prepared to move into their tracks the moment the chair has picked them up. Determine beforehand over which shoulder you will look for the chair. If you start moving early, you should have plenty of time to get into position.

2) Once in position, look backwards, over your shoulder, to see the chair coming. Always look to the side of the supporting pole. If the chair has a center pole, look over your inside shoulder. If the chair has outside supports, look over your outside shoulder *(Figure 77).*

3) Hold your ski poles in the hand away from the supporting pole of the chair. Use your outside hand for center-pole chairs, your inside hand for chairs with outside supports. In either case, hold the poles as far away from your body as possible with an outstretched arm. This will prevent you or your partner from tangling with them. Hold the poles in the middle of the shaft, not at the grips.

4) Grasp the front edge of the chair seat with your free hand—the hand without the ski poles. This will prevent the chair from hitting the backs of your legs. An alternative is to grasp the *front* of the supporting pole of the chair. Some skiers wrap their arm around the supporting pole, instead of grabbing the pole on its front side. This works well for experienced lift riders, but it takes considerable practice to do smoothly. The lift attendant will usually assist you by helping hold back the chair. However, sometimes an attendant is not there. To play safe, always plan to use your own hand to check the movement of the chair seat before it hits the calves of your legs.

5) Once you have grasped the seat with your hand, sit down quickly, getting the weight off your feet as soon

Getting on the Lift

Figure 77

In getting on the lift: **1)** look over the shoulder of the supporting pole of the chair; **2)** extend that hand to grasp either the seat or the supporting pole of the chair; and **3)** hold your poles in the other hand far in front of you. As soon as you touch the chair with your hand, sit down quickly, getting your weight off your feet and in the chair as soon as possible. In the above photo, the skier on the right is still looking over his shoulder as he grasps the supporting pole. The skier on the left has already straightened his head; he has a firm grasp on the supporting pole and is beginning to sit down. (Copper Mountain Photo by Rick Godin.)

as you can. It is unnecessary to lift your feet up, as this will happen automatically. If your weight is on your seat early, your skis will be unweighted and present no problem. However, to keep your weight on the skis too long is to court disaster. As the chair lift progresses, it raises the chair away from the ground, making it harder to get your seat in the proper place. Therefore, to repeat, sitting down in the chair as quickly as possible is the key to proper loading.

6 To unload, hold both poles in the outside hand, regardless of where the supporting poles are. Place your other hand, the inside hand, against the edge of the seat.

7) Rest your feet on the unloading platform as soon as you can, but do not rush to stand up. Instead, move your seat forward in the chair and prepare to push off with your hand.

8) Most unloading platforms are flat for several feet and then slant downhill. Wait to stand up until you feel your skis begin to head downhill. Standing up too soon causes the chair to push the backs of your legs until you've reached the decline. This can cause a fall. Instead, wait until you reach the decline, stand up quickly, and push off the chair with your inside hand.

9) Before you reach the top, ask your partner in which direction he or she will head when unloading. This can avoid a collision.

27

Skiing in the Wilderness

Unpatrolled Areas

In the mountains, outside the maintained slopes of developed ski areas, skiers are exposed to a variety of hazards, some of which can be life-threatening. Cross-country (Nordic) skiers who are touring, as well as downhill (Alpine) skiers who are seeking untracked powder slopes, should be familiar with these risks and be prepared to handle them *before* they arise. Statistics reveal that since 1910, the majority of people who died in avalanches in the United States were Alpine or Nordic skiers.

Most of the dangers are the result of becoming lost, stranded, or buried because of injury, bad weather, or avalanches. The remoteness of an area and its terrain will determine the equipment and preparation required.

Equipment

The equipment to carry into the wilderness will depend on the likelihood of avalanches and of being stranded overnight. When this is a possibility, a backpack with the proper supplies is essential, as it should provide sufficient resources to survive overnight in a snow cave in the most adverse conditions.

Equipment List

- Extra clothing to stay warm in cold weather—especially mittens and socks
- Wool scarf
- Quick high-energy foods, such as dried fruit, raisins, candy
- Space blankets

- Portable snow shovel
- Avalanche cord (50-foot nylon rope) dyed red—the color recommended by the U.S. Forest Service
- Candles and matches in a waterproof container
- Unbreakable container of water
- Flashlight
- Flares
- First-aid kit including:
  Adhesive tape (2-inch width)
  Band-Aids of different sizes
  Gauze squares (3×3 or 4×4)
  Razor blade or scissors
  Safety pins
  Four-inch Ace bandage
  Small cake of soap
  Tweezers
  Plastic air splints (one arm, one leg)
  Arm sling
  Leather case to hold the above (metal rusts)
  In avalanche areas, also carry a collapsible probe and electronic transceivers

---

Going for Help

If someone is injured and cannot travel, the immediate threat is cold exposure. If possible, move the person to a sheltered area. Try to improvise a barrier to shield him or her from the wind and blowing snow.

1) If there are more than two people, one should stay with the victim.

2) In larger groups, send at least three people to seek aid, especially if the route is long or dangerous. Should one become injured, there will still be others to continue the journey.

3) Take time to observe landmarks in the rescue area so that it can be found again when returning with help. Shiny objects that can reflect light are useful as extra markers.

4) While time is important, a short delay in rescue will usually not affect the medical outcome. Therefore, proceed for assistance with caution. Should the persons seeking help become injured, the whole party could be in serious jeopardy.

28. Avalanches

Consultants: Misha Plam, Knox Williams, and M. Martinelli, Jr.

If you are a downhill skier and ski only on the slopes of maintained ski areas, your experience with avalanches is probably limited to reading signs which warn "Keep Out—Avalanche Area" or to reading news clippings such as the following:

A 26-year-old man was killed when he and two companions, who were on a cross-country skiing trip, were hit by an avalanche in the mountains. The accident occurred in the same spot where a school administrator died in a snowslide four years ago. The survivors were rescued by two other skiers who witnessed the slide and promptly dug them out from the snow. It was solely due to the efforts of these young men that the survivors are alive today.

(From the Denver Post, *January 7, 1979.)*

If you ski in places that are not patrolled or if you cross-country ski in the mountains, you can be exposed to the dangers of avalanches or snowslides. Knowing something about them can help you save the life of another skier, or even your own.

Causes of Avalanches

An avalanche is a rapidly descending mass of snow and ice caused by the accumulation of snow on a mountainside following snow and wind storms. The snowpacks which form are composed of numerous grains of snow, held together by cohesive bonds of varying strength, depending on the temperature, wind, and other weather conditions. Snow on a slope is also under the constant force of gravity trying to pull it downhill. As snow piles higher it becomes heavier, and eventually, under certain conditions, the snowpack may slide.

Most avalanches occur on slopes with pitches of 30°

to 45°, the same pitches that provide the best powder skiing. Steeper slopes usually do not hold enough snow to form a large slide. Avalanches have occurred on slopes of less than 30°, but only under extremely unstable conditions. Other contributing factors to avalanches are large accumulations and rapid increases of fresh snow, changing temperatures, strong winds, and exposure to solar radiation. In general, avalanches tend to occur above timberline on steep, open, snow-laden slopes, either during or within twenty-four hours of a storm, or in clear, warm weather. They occur on south-facing sun-drenched slopes, especially on spring afternoons. As a safety precaution, many mountain areas (for example, in Colorado, Utah, and Washington) issue avalanche warnings when several of these conditions are present. These warning should be heeded. Each year many people lose their lives in avalanches because they ignored the advice of the mountain weather forecasters. Unfortunately, the conditions for good powder skiing and avalanches are very similar.

General Safety Precautions in Avalanche Areas

You should never ski alone in unpatrolled areas, regardless of your skiing ability. When skiing with a group, don't separate too far apart. If you should fall and be injured, your location may easily be lost.

Try to avoid skiing down known avalanche paths, particularly at times of high danger, such as after heavy snows, periods of high winds, and rapid temperature rises. Avalanche paths can sometimes be recognized by their vegetation patterns. The path and its run-out zone (bottom) will be barren or covered by aspen trees, but will be free of large evergreens *(Figure 78).* However, avalanche locations can also look deceptively safe *(Figure 79).* History has shown that avalanches tend to recur in the same locations and that the best safety precaution is to ski with someone who is familiar with the area and the known avalanche spots.

There are times when you may be forced to cross an avalanche path. The safest route is over the top, by way of the ridges, while the second safest is along the valley floor. At times, both of these routes are unreachable. The next choice is to cross the path as high as possible, to keep most of the potential avalanche be-

Typical Avalanche Path

Figure 78

The open path in the left half of this picture is typical of an avalanche track. This cut through an evergreen forest must be regarded as a potential slide area, particularly at times of high avalanche danger. (Photo by U.S. Forest Service.)

low you. Finally, if you must cross in the middle, try to pick the narrowest part so that your distance to safety will be short if the slope should begin sliding.

When camping in the mountains, common sense dictates that you should not establish your campsite at the foot of an avalanche zone. Yet every once in a while people are buried in an avalanche because they thought it wouldn't happen to them and were careless enough to camp in such a spot.

Despite all efforts to eliminate avalanche dangers, it is impossible to guarantee that you won't be caught in one. While most avalanches begin with the first skier on the slope, it sometimes won't slide until the second, third, or even the tenth skier has descended. Potential avalanches are sometimes dynamited to release avalanches when no one is on the slope. Yet even after dynamiting, a slope that was safe earlier in the day may become hazardous with changing weather.

Figure 79

A Typical Avalanche Slope

This rather heavily timbered slope appears quite inviting to powder skiers after a new snow, and is skied frequently. However, the trees are not dense enough to stabilize the snow. During the past several years, many skiers have been killed in this innocuous-looking area. This is an excellent example of how looks can be deceiving. The danger cannot be seen. It is known only to those who are familiar with the area. (From the Floral Park avalanche area, Berthoud Pass, Colorado. Photo by the U.S. Forest Service.)

Precautions When Crossing an Avalanche

At times an avalanche path cannot be avoided and must be crossed. You should observe certain precautions before entering it.

Always ski across or down a dangerous slope **one at a time.** The risk of an avalanche increases when more than one person simultaneously disturbs the equilibrium of the snowpack. If several skiers are traversing a path, they should all stay in the same tracks to avoid additional disturbances. If you are skiing down a dangerous slope, try to stay near the side of the path rather than the center; should a slide occur, it will be easier for you to ski out of the avalanche by reaching the side.

Before starting, remove any straps on your equipment that would prevent you from releasing it. Specifically, take the pole straps off your wrists and undo the safety straps on your ski. If you are wearing a backpack, loosen the straps and hip belt so the pack can be dumped quickly if you are knocked over.

Your clothing should be buttoned, zipped, or tied, and your head should be covered. If you are buried in an avalanche, you will survive longer if the snow remains outside your clothing and does not touch your skin. It is also a good idea to wear a scarf tied loosely around your neck; you can pull it over your nose and mouth if you are caught in a slide.

If you are carrying rescue devices—and you should be carrying at least one—be sure they are in proper order. Check your electronic receiver in the morning before tying it around your neck. It should be worn inside your clothing so that it won't be torn away.

Avalanche cords are used by some people even though they are cumbersome. Tie one end of a red-colored cord around your waist, leaving the other end free to trail behind you. This should float on top of the snow if you are buried. It is not a guarantee, but it can be helpful.

Plan your crossing to take advantage of safety islands in the terrain, such as clumps of trees or rock protrusions. Ski towards these, and just above them. When skiing in open bowls with steep pitches where avalanches might occur, try not to stop in the middle of the slope or at the base of the steep pitch. Ski a couple of hundred feet out onto the flatter area beyond the steep pitch. If an avalanche begins, it will pile the greatest depth of snow at the point where the steep slope blends into the flatter area. If you stand in that place, you will be buried in the deepest spot.

What to Do If You Are Caught in an Avalanche

1) First, attempt to ski out to the side. If you are knocked over, throw away your poles, skis, and backpack immediately.
2) Call out to others in your group to watch you so that if you are buried they will know where to begin their search.
3) Pull up the scarf from around your neck and place it over your nose and mouth, holding it in place with the lower edge of your goggles.
4) Try to stay near the surface of the snow by a swimming motion.
5) If your swimming is not working, cover your nose and mouth with both hands and keep them there. This

will provide your best chance of forming an air pocket over your face in which to breathe while awaiting rescue.

6) If you can move when the slide has stopped, try to dig yourself out *immediately,* before it settles. If you cannot move, lie quietly, as your oxygen supply is limited. Strenuous but futile efforts will only burn up oxygen.

7) If you are digging out, be sure to dig upwards. To determine direction, spit forward or let saliva drip from your mouth. If the saliva falls back in your face, you are facing upwards. If it falls away, you are facing downwards and must dig out in the opposite direction.

8) Shouting to rescuers will not help, since sound is buried in the snow. It is normal to hear sounds from above the ground. Do not try to answer unless you are certain you are within a few inches of the surface. As a rule, shouting only consumes your much-needed energy.

9) If you are skiing down a slope when an avalanche begins above you, *keep on skiing.* Head both downhill and towards the side of the slope, preferably toward trees, if there are any. Nothing will be gained by stopping. Many people have successfully skied away from an oncoming avalanche by remaining calm and continuing to ski.

Electronic Transceivers

Anyone skiing in a potential avalanche area should wear a battery-powered electronic transceiver and carry a shovel. In addition, it is essential that all skiers in the group be equipped with similar transceivers, as it does little good to be buried with an electronic device if there is no one around who can hear the signal!

A transceiver is an instrument capable of sending and receiving a signal, although it does only one at a time. The instrument is worn around the neck and is always maintained in the "send" position. When someone has been buried in an avalanche, all instruments in the search party must immediately be turned to the "receive" position so they can detect the signal of the buried person.

There are different manufacturers of transceivers (the American-made Skadi and Austrian Pieps are two examples). Each unit sends and receives the same specified radio frequency. Units from different manufacturers, but on the same frequency, can be used interchangeably. However, units on different frequencies will not hear each other's signals. Before starting a trip, always check transceivers against each other to make sure their batteries are charged and they are all on the same frequency.

Procedure for Avalanche Search

Below is a suggested protocol for carrying out a search when someone is caught in an avalanche. Before skiing in potential avalanche areas, every skier should know this procedure thoroughly *and* should carry out practice drills with a transceiver. Do this by having one person bury a signal device in the snow and another person use his or her detector to find it.

Searching with Transceivers

1) Don't panic—take a few seconds to organize. If you are in a group, one person should take charge and the others follow his or her orders. Discipline is important in an avalanche search. Lives are lost by wasting minutes, but not seconds. Most people buried in the snow have at least a few minutes of oxygen. Sample statistics of avalanche burials revealed that all seventeen people who were found within 8 minutes of burial survived. Most of these people had been buried over 5 minutes. Fifty percent of those found within 30 minutes survived. After 30 minutes, the death rate increased rapidly, but there were a few survivors who had been buried for several hours *(Figure 80).*
2) Beforehand, read the manufacturer's recommendations for the range of each instrument. Switch all electronic units to receive, and the volume to maximum. *This step is vital.*
3) It takes less time to walk downhill than uphill. When above the victim, begin searching from above.
4) Mark the point where the skier was last seen. For markers use ski poles, skis, or pieces of clothing.
5) If appropriate, have one person stand guard to watch for another slide.
6) Begin a straight line of searchers at the level where the victim was last seen.
7) All searchers should move down the mountain in unison, in a straight line. Stop about every ten feet and slowly rotate the transceiver in each direction.
8) When a signal is heard at maximum volume, reduce the volume setting until it can barely be heard.

Figure 80

Survival of Avalanche Victims

This graph depicts the percentage of people who have survived after being buried in an avalanche. Fifty percent of those who were rescued 30 minutes after burial were still alive. Almost all victims uncovered within a few minutes survived. The survival rate falls rapidly with time, but even after being buried for a few hours an occasional victim has been found alive. (Reproduced by permission from: *The Snowy Torrents: Avalanche Accidents in the U.S., 1967–71,* William Knox, 1975)

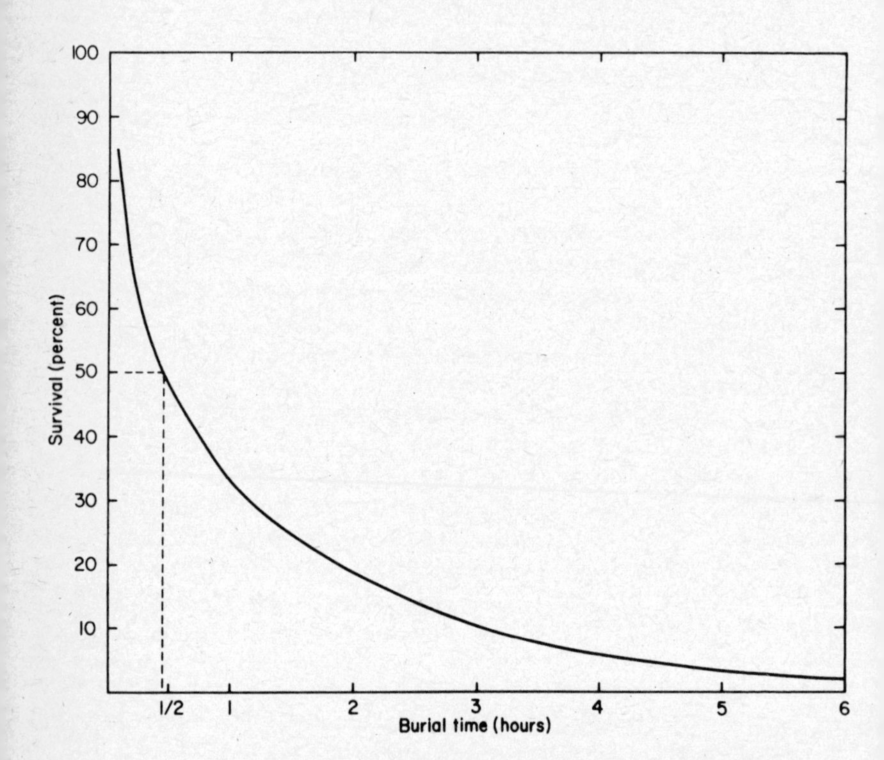

Notify the other searchers in the line. Stay on the lowest volume which still permits a signal to be heard.

9) When the signal gets weaker, the victim has been passed. Place a marker in the snow at this point and remember the signal level.

10) Walk in the reverse direction, uphill, with the transceiver on the same volume level. The signal will first get louder, then softer. When it reaches the same signal level as before, place another marker in the snow.

11) Estimate the distance between the two markers, then walk to the midpoint. From there, walk a perpendicular line in one direction or the other. If the sound gets softer, you are walking in the wrong direction. If the sound gets louder, you are walking in the right direction. Stop when it is at its loudest. Repeat the procedure on this level and set two more markers. Walk up and down the hill between these two markers to the point where the signal is loudest.

12) Before digging at this spot, pinpoint the location on your hands and knees with the transceiver on its lowest volume setting.

13) While digging, one person should continue using the transceiver to verify the location.

14) *Note:* Turn the volume control of the transceiver only when standing still. Movement can cause false signals.

15) *Note:* A double beeping tone means two electronic units are transmitting. Either there are two people buried or one of the searchers has not switched his transceiver to receive.

Searching with Probes

If transceivers are not available, long metal or wooden probes are another method for searching for an avalanche victim. Probers should follow an organized pattern of movement down the slope, just as with transceivers. The probe must be forced into the snow every foot, in hopes of hitting resistance, which could be the buried skier. Probing is tedious, slow, very difficult, and usually futile. However, it should be used when other methods are not available. It can save a life.

Avalanche Dogs

Avalanche dogs, which have been trained to pick up the human scent, can usually locate a skier in an avalanche faster than electronic signalers. When these animals arrive on the scene of an avalanche, ask all people to leave the area so as to not distract the dog. Once the dog locates the victim, the searchers can join in the dig. But trained dogs usually must be transported to the avalanche area, which takes precious time. Searchers on the scene should begin search efforts and continue them until the dogs arrive.

29 First Aid

Evaluation and Planning

Before treating an injury on a ski slope, take a few moments to evaluate the situation. Examine the injured person where he or she is lying and check for the three emergency situations: bleeding, stoppage of breathing, stoppage of heartbeat.

Inspect the body for obvious signs of bleeding. If the person can talk, he or she is breathing. If the victim is unconscious, observe the chest for motion or hold a hand or your ear over the nose and mouth to detect signs of air moving. Feel for a pulse in the wrist or the neck. If there is major bleeding, immediately apply direct pressure. If respiration or the heartbeat has stopped, cardiopulmonary resuscitation must be started. If the pulse exists but is weak, a state of "shock," or low blood pressure, may be present. Not much can be done for this except keeping the skier lying down and as warm as possible.

Once the life-threatening conditions have been evaluated, carefully examine the injured part. If an extremity or the spine is in pain, gently run your hand over the involved area, pressing against the skin every few inches (called palpation). If one area is more tender than the others, it often means that there is an injury at this spot. It might or might not be serious, but this is difficult to determine on the slope. It is best to play safe and handle it as a serious injury until a more thorough examination by a qualified person is possible.

In maintained ski areas, send someone to call the ski patrol. Stand a pair of skis in the shape of an X above the injured person so other skiers will ski around the spot. If you are in the wilderness where there is no ski patrol, you must send for help. Plan the trip carefully. If you prepared for your wilderness skiing properly, you will have some emergency supplies with you. (See Chapter 27.)

Lacerations

Direct pressure over the bleeding point, with a clean handkerchief or similar pad, will stop most bleeding in 5 to 30 minutes. Pressure can be maintained by wrapping a bandage, scarf, handkerchief, or whatever else is available over the pressure pad. Leave the bandage in place until you arrive at the first-aid station, since removing the dressing from the cut can tear away the blood clot and renew the bleeding.

Sprains

A sprain is a torn ligament around a joint. Most ski sprains are the result of the body's weight being thrown against a turned or twisted ankle or knee. All sprains produce pain when the joint is moved, and severe sprains may cause swelling and discoloration from torn blood vessels. When the ligament is only partially torn (mild sprain), the damaged area will be sore to the touch, but the joint will feel solid. If the ligament is completely torn, the joint may be unstable; that is, it will bend beyond its normal limits. Because it can be difficult to differentiate a sprain from a fracture or dislocation, sprains should be treated as if they were fractures until a medical opinion is obtained. Sprains are treated with an ice pack for the first several hours. This may help diminish the swelling and reduce the pain. After 24 hours, heat will be of greater value, as it promotes more blood supply to the area to enhance healing.

Pain is a symptom, and the degree of pain is often, although not always, an indication of the severity of the sprain. If pain is mild, and the joint is stable, you may slowly try to put weight on the leg. If the pain becomes severe, or the joint weak, *do not try* to "walk away the pain." Splint the leg and avoid walking on it until it has been evaluated medically. A partially torn ligament may tear completely if it is stressed too far.

Muscle Strains

A strain is an injury in which the muscle fibers have been stretched or torn. In skiing, the muscles most commonly strained are the calf muscles, behind the lower leg, the muscles lying next to the shinbone, and the inner thigh muscles. Strains result from overexerting a muscle by making it do more work than it has been trained to do; they can be prevented by proper muscle conditioning. There is no treatment for a strain except rest. When a muscle starts to hurt while you are skiing, it is best to either stop skiing or take it easy for the remainder of that day. Continuing to exercise strenuously may result in a sore or ruptured muscle which can be disabling for several days or longer. However, as a rule, no serious damage results from muscle strains.

Dislocations

A dislocation occurs when the end of a bone is separated from its joint. This can only occur if the ligaments and other supporting structures of a joint have been torn or badly stretched. The shoulder is the most common joint dislocated by skiers. Others are the kneecap, the fingers, and especially the thumb.

1) *Shoulder dislocations.* These should be treated with a sling, to hold the arm against the chest until medical treatment is available. In general, unless the circulation to the hand is cut off, immediate corrective treatment is not essential. A few hours' delay will be uncomfortable, but will cause no harm.

2) *Kneecap dislocations.* A dislocation of the kneecap results from a blow to the knee. You can diagnose it by seeing if the kneecap has shifted its position towards the outside of the knee. If in doubt, compare its position to that of the good knee. Kneecap dislocations are treated by pushing the kneecap back in place. This is best done by holding the leg out straight, so the knee joint is not bent, and pushing the kneecap back into its correct position.

3) *Finger dislocations.* These are treated by pulling the finger firmly in the line of normal orientation, with the finger held out straight. After correcting a finger dislocation, the finger should be splinted, or taped to an adjacent finger, to prevent recurrent dislocation and to permit the joint capsule to heal. Medical attention should be sought even if the dislocation has been corrected on the slope. Small fractures can accompany dislocations, and their presence can only be detected by X-ray.

Fractures

Most ski fractures occur in the lower leg. Pain is the classical symptom of a fracture, and usually, though not always, the pain is severe. Some fractures are easy to diagnose, while others are detectable only by X-ray. A few signs of a fracture are listed on the next page.

1) *A bump or deformity* on the skin can indicate a fracture. If the deformity is near a joint it could indicate a dislocation, with or without a fracture. Comparing the injured with the uninjured limb may be necessary to be certain whether there is a deformity.
2) *Exposed ends of bone* in the middle of an open wound is the most obvious sign of a fracture.
3) *Pain and tenderness* to touch are almost always present with a fracture. However, these signs are also seen with simple bone bruises, sprains, and strains. If no bump or deformity is present over the tender area, an X-ray is needed to diagnose a fracture.
4) *Swelling and discoloration,* like pain and tenderness, often accompany fractures, but may also occur with bruises and sprains. Injuries showing these signs should be regarded and treated as fractures until X-rays are taken to be certain.
5) *The sound of a crack or snap* heard by the skier may well be the sound of a bone breaking.

The first-aid management for skiers with fractures or suspected fractures is the same:

1) Keep the skier warm, using scarfs, sweaters, jackets, or blankets.

2) Send for help.

3) Stand a pair of skis erect in the snow in the shape of an X so other skiers will know someone needs help.

4) If there is significant bleeding, control it with a pressure bandage.

5) Straighten out a severely angulated fracture by pulling it straight in the line of the long axis of the extremity.

6) If bone is exposed, cover it with something clean.

7) Apply a splint to the limb before moving the skier. The splint can be anything that will prevent the extremity from bending. Some splints are stiff, such as pieces of wood, tree limbs, or even skis. Other splints, of flexible materials, also work effectively. Inflatable plastic air splints are excellent.

8) The splint should extend beyond the joints above and below the fracture. For a lower-leg injury, the splint should begin above the knee and reach to below the ankle.

9) The splint can be fixed with rope, handkerchiefs, scarfs, or anything tied around the extremity.

10) If possible, bring the stretcher or sled up to the injured skier. Three or four people should lift and transfer the skier to it.

Head and Spine Injuries

Head and spinal injuries can be very serious, and at times life-threatening. Their diagnosis may or may not be obvious from the skier's appearance. Sensations of weakness or tingling in the arms or legs, even for short periods, may be the only signs of a serious injury. No treatment can be given on the slope except cardiopulmonary resuscitation if the heart and lungs have stopped. This is a true emergency and must be treated immediately. Mouth-to-mouth resuscitation and chest massage can only be performed by people who have had at least a first-aid course in these techniques—a good reason why all skiers should take such a course.

Moving someone who has sustained a head or spinal injury requires extreme care. Immediately after the accident, the skier should be stretched out flat and kept in that position until help arrives. Bending the neck or back could result in total paralysis. If you must move the injured person before help arrives, pull him or her along the ground by grabbing the collar of the clothing behind the neck and dragging the body over the ground without lifting the head or bending the neck. When help arrives, move the skier onto the stretcher with the neck and spine maintained straight.

Heart Attacks

The sudden onset of chest pain and shortness of breath may or may not be the beginning of a heart attack. Anyone developing such symptoms on a ski slope should be handled as though he or she is having a heart attack until medical evaluation is available.

On the slope, the skier with chest pain should sit or lie down, to expend as little energy as possible. The correct position is the one in which it is easiest to breathe. Keep the person warm by covering him or her with any pieces of clothing available. When calling for help, ask the rescue party to bring a portable oxygen tank. This is about all that can be done on the slope unless the heart stops. If this occurs, chest massage and mouth-to-mouth resuscitation (CPR) should be practiced immediately. As just mentioned, cardiopulmonary resuscitation must be administered by someone with training.

Consultant: Hal O'Leary

Handicapped Skiers

To some extent all skiers have handicaps. They wear skis because their feet are too short. They wear stiff boots because their ankles are too flexible. Another common handicap is a psychological one—fear. The fear of falling and the fear of injury are drawbacks that most skiers must overcome. Therefore, a significant part of learning to ski is learning to deal with handicaps.

Skiing is not only a strenuous sport, it is also an excellent form of physical therapy and rehabilitation for a variety of physical handicaps. People with multiple sclerosis, post-polio weakness, cerebral plasy, spina bifida, amputations, blindness, deafness, and many other disabilities are finding skiing enjoyable and exciting. Skiing has proved to be effective and instrumental in improving the physical and mental attitudes of many handicapped individuals.

Amputees

The skier with one leg has a handicap that is surmountable. The use of two outriggers on the tips of Canadian crutches gives the one-legged skier good balance *(Figure 81)*. This three-track skiing method is based on the same basic skills of skiing as mentioned in Part I: edge control, balance, rotation, and unweighting. Knee angulation and steering are stressed. Down-unweighting is much easier for the one-legged skier than other choices.

Figure 81

Poles Provide Balance

The amputee skier must rely heavily on the ski poles for balance. The points of the poles are replaced with short ski tips which act as outriggers. In this way the arms can supply the balance that is usually provided by the second leg. (Photo from the Winter Park Handicap Ski Program, Hal O'Leary, Director.)

The amputee skier has a few specific health concerns.

1) *Care of the hands.* Using outriggers, the three-track skier puts constant pressure on his hands. This reduces the blood supply to the hands, which tend to get cold easily. Mittens with good insulation will provide more warmth than gloves. If the hands become cold or the fingers numb, time should be taken to increase their circulation. Some hand-warming exercises are swinging the arms vigorously and shaking the hands from the wrists. If the hands still do not warm up, it is wisest to go inside until they have regained feeling.

2) *Stump care.* The tip of the amputated extremity often has limited blood supply. As a result, it needs extra protection in cold weather. The use of one or two wool socks will provide additional warmth. Padding over the stump end will protect it from bruising as well as give it a little extra heat insulation. Frequent movement of the stump on the chair lift will also help keep it warm.

3) *Fatigue.* Fatigue occurs quickly in one-legged skiers because the energy required to maintain balance is much higher. As a result, amputees require more rest stops than other skiers. It is important for amputees to realize that their tendency to get fatigued is quite normal. A pre-season conditioning program, to build strength and endurance in the good leg, will improve stamina.

Blind Skiers

Consultant: Hal O'Leary

For the blind, skiing offers a unique medium to fulfill a need for adventure, recreation, exercise, freedom, and self-respect. Blind skiers attain a sense of direction by feeling the contour of the hill, through which they are able to sense the fall line. The blind derive enormous satisfaction from skiing because it permits them to move with speed and grace. In addition, it offers them an unusual opportunity to join the mainstream of life by participating in such a vigorous physical activity on the same level as sighted people.

On the slopes, blind people must be accompanied by a guide. For safety, they wear signs indicating that they are blind so sighted skiers will not run into them *(Figure 82).*

When skiing, blind people should wear protective glasses, even though they have no vision. The sun and wind can still damage the outer layers of their eyes, causing the same kind of pain sighted skiers can experience.

Senior Citizens—You're Never Too Old to Ski

Consultant: Dr. Albert Guggenheim

While skiing is generally regarded as a sport for younger people, it is not unusual to see senior citizens on the slopes. Most of these people learned to ski when they were younger. While it is difficult to learn to ski after fifty or sixty, it is not impossible. However, there are certain limitations that should be observed. Below are a few suggestions for senior skiers:

1) Don't be ashamed to ask for assistance in putting on boots and skis.

Figure 82

Blind Skiers Wear Signs

Blind skiers wear signs indicating their lack of vision and always ski with a guide. The blind attain a sense of direction by the feel of the contour of the hill from which they are able to perceive the fall line.

2) Don't ski alone.

3) After a fall, ask for assistance in getting up.

4) Do not ski without the permission of your physician if you have heart disease, lung disease, or high blood pressure.

5) Do not try to exercise at age seventy as you did when you were forty or fifty. Your endurance will be less, particularly at high altitudes.

Downhill Skiing and Racing

Joubert, G.: *Teach Yourself to Ski.* Aspen Ski Masters, Aspen, Colorado, 1970.

Witherell, W.: *How the Racers Ski.* W. W. Norton, New York, 1972.

Cross-Country Skiing

Caldwell, J.: *Cross-Country Skiing Today.* Stephen Greene Press, Brattleboro, Vermont, 1977.

Tokle, A., and M. Luray: *The Complete Guide to Cross-Country Skiing and Touring,* rev. ed. Vintage Books, New York, 1977.

Conditioning

Cooper, K. H.: *The New Aerobics.* M. Evans and Co., New York, 1970.

Fixx, J. F.: *The Complete Book of Running.* Random House, New York, 1977.

Foss, M. L., and J. G. Garrick: *Ski Conditioning.* John Wiley & Sons, New York, 1978.

Mountain Medicine

Darvill, F. T., Jr.: *Mountaineering Medicine: A Wilderness Medical Guide,* 8th ed. SKI: Skagit Mountain Rescue Unit, Mount Vernon, Washington, 1977.

Avalanches

Perla, R. I., and M. Martinelli, Jr.: *Avalanche Handbook,* U.S. Department of Agriculture Handbook, U.S. Government Printing Office, Washington, D.C., 1975.

Williams, K.: *The Snowy Torrents: Avalanche Accidents in the United States 1967–71.* USDA Forest Service General Technical Report, 1975. Room 8, Rocky Mountain Forest and Range Experiment Station, Fort Collins, Colorado 80521, 1975.

Handicaps

O'Leary, H.: *The Winter Park Amputee Ski Teaching System.* Box 313, Winter Park, Colorado, 1974.

Aerobic Exercises Any activity that lasts more than one minute and therefore utilizes more oxygen than is required at rest.

Acute Cerebral Edema Unconsciousness from swelling around the brain which can be seen as a result of a sudden increase in altitude.

Acute Mountain Sickness Shortness of breath due to high altitude.

Alpine Skiing Cross-country skiing.

Angulation Bending one or more joints of the body.

Knee Angulation (Also called *cranking*) Bending the knee joint sideways to set the ski on an edge. This action of the knee is possible only when the knee joint is *flexed*. Knee angulation is the most important mechanism for edge control.

Hip Angulation Pushing the hips uphill and leaning the shoulders downhill to set the skis on their edges.

Anticipation Facing the upper body (the shoulders and head) downhill before a turn is made. The upper body thus "anticipates" the next turn.

Avalanche A rapidly descending mass of snow and ice on a mountainside.

Avalanche Cord A colored piece of rope, usually 50 feet long, that is tied around the waist when skiing down avalanche-prone slopes.

Avalement A French word meaning swallowing. This is an advanced technique of turning smoothly over moguls at high speeds, but can also be used on smooth slopes. Avalement combines the basic elements of leg retraction with jetting and early edging by banking. A compensatory flexion of the waist accompanies avalement.

Banking Leaning inward against centrifugal force. Banking results in setting the skis on their inside edges. It is thus a form of edge control. Banking on skis is similar to banking on a bicycle.

Camber The flexibility of a ski. The upward curve in a ski when lying flat. When the ski is set on its edge and the body's weight pushes against the center of the ski, the ski's curve reverses. This is called *reverse camber*. The ski's reverse camber is used to carve a turn.

Cardio-Pulmonary Resuscitation (CPR) Reviving a person whose heart or lungs have stopped working.

Carving Completing a turn by following the arc produced in the ski when it is edged and weighted. The carved turn is a turn that follows the direction in which the ski tip is pointing. The opposite of a carved turn is a skidded turn, in which the turn is led by the side of the ski rather than the tip.

Checking Reducing speed by a quick edgeset. Used for slowing down and stopping.

Christy A parallel turn which ends with a skid. The term was born in the town of Christiana, now called Oslo, in Norway. This term is seldom used in modern skiing.

Cranking The same as knee angulation. Rolling the knees to the side to change the direction of the ski by edging.

Edging Rolling the skis onto their edges. Edging, or edge control, permits turning, speed control, and stopping. Edging the skis is performed by knee angulation, by hip angulation, or by banking.

Edge Change A method of initiating a parallel turn by rolling the knees, or banking, from one side to the other. This changes the direction in which the skis are pointing by switching from one set of edges to the other set.

Electronic Transceivers Devices used to find people who are buried in avalanches.

Extension Straightening out a flexed joint. When unweighting, by either leg retraction or down-unweighting, the knees become tightly flexed (or bent). From this position, the legs must be partially straightened, by extending them.

Fall Line The shortest and the steepest path down a hill.

Flexion Bending of a joint. A correct skiing stance will include flexion of the knee, ankle, and hip joints.

Foot Twist or Swivel Rotation of the feet (or legs) to initiate a parallel turn.

Friction Plates Smooth surfaces fixed to skis that permit a foot to slide freely out of a binding.

Frostbite Injury to the hands and feet from exposure to cold temperatures.

Herringbone Technique for walking uphill with ski tips pointing upward.

Hip Projection A form of hip rotation in which the outside hip is lifted up and rotated in the direction of the turn. Elevating the hip flattens the skis against the slope to make it a little easier to pivot them. Hip projection must be stopped (blocked) early in the turn to permit edging of the skis for control. When blocking, the hips must be pushed inward, toward the center of the turn. Hip projection is reserved for "survival" in difficult circumstances, particularly in heavy or crusty snow.

Hypothermia Lowered body temperature due to prolonged exposure to cold temperatures.

Inside Leg or Ski The leg or ski nearest the center of a turn.

Lateral Sideways. A lateral movement is a movement to the side. Lateral slippage means sliding the edges of the skis to the side (or sideslipping).

Leverage The effect of the skier's weight when it is transferred ahead of or behind the center of the ski.

Forward Leverage (Also called *forward weight transfer*) Shifting some of the body's weight forward, to the balls of the feet.

Backward Leverage (Also called *backward weight transfer*) Returning the weight to the middle of the ski (or the heels) after it has been transferred forward. It can also mean putting more weight on the heels.

Jetting Jetting is a quick thrust forward of the feet and legs resulting from the release of stretched muscles. Flexing the knees deeply and angulating them to the side stretches the extensor muscles of the legs. When unweighting releases these muscles, their rebound thrusts the feet forward.

Leg Retraction A method of unweighting performed by tightening the abdominal and back muscles and lifting the knees upwards.

Nordic Skiing Downhill skiing.

Outside Leg or Ski The leg or ski away from the center of a turn.

Parallel Turn A turn initiated by changing the direction of both skis simultaneously. In order to turn both legs at the same time it is usually necessary to momentarily remove the body's weight from the feet (unweighting). The two methods of initiating parallel turns are edge change and rotation.

Platform The position of tight compression of the legs produced by both knee flexion and knee angulation. This provides a stable springboard from which to launch a turn.

Pre-turn (Also called *counter-turn*) Turning the skis uphill just prior to turning downhill.

Pulmonary Edema Shortness of breath and fluid accumulation in the lungs.

Pulse The number of heartbeats per minute.

Rotation Turning the body around its long axis. The body's long axis is comparable to a flagpole running from the top of the head to a point between the two feet. A twisting movement of the feet, knees, hips, or shoulders will turn the body around its axis. Anticipation is rotation of the shoulders before the turn.

Side-cut or Side-camber The curve in the side of the ski which results in the tip and tail being wider than the midsection of the ski. The side-cut permits the ski to carve on a packed slope when weighted and properly edged.

Sideslipping Lateral movement of the ski. The side of the ski leads the ski straight down the fall line. Sideslipping is performed by releasing the edges to partially flatten the bottoms of the skis against the slope.

Skidding Completing a turn by combining sideslipping with rotation of the skis. The tails of the skis slip faster than the tips, causing the tails to rotate around the tips. In skidding the turn is led by the side of the ski, whereas in carving the turn is led by the tip of the ski.

Snowplow or Wedge A V-shaped position of the skis with the ski tips lying together and the tails pushed apart. This position is used primarily for slowing down or stopping on narrow trails by setting the skis on their inside edges.

Steering Changing the direction of the skis gradually by applying the forces of both knee angulation and foot rotation to weighted skis.

Stem Turn Derived from the German word *stemmen,* meaning to push against or brace. Stemming is initiating a turn by pushing the tail of one ski outward so the ski is pointing in the new direction, rolling that ski onto its inside edge, then transferring weight to it. The stem turn is a one-legged turn. It is performed by transferring weight from one leg to the other, and therefore does not require unweighting.

Traversing Traveling across a hill perpendicular to the fall line, with no lateral slippage.

Unweighting A sudden removal of the body's weight from the feet. This can occur in four ways.

1) UP-unweighting—a sudden hop upwards.

2) DOWN-unweighting—a quick drop of the seat.

3) Leg retracting—tightening the abdominal muscles and lifting the knees up.

4) Using a bump or mogul—skiing over irregular terrain automatically unweights.

Wedeln A technique of turning rapidly in which the turning action is performed by the lower half of the body while the upper half remains facing downhill. The word *wedeln* is German for wiggle.

Weighting Placing weight on one or both feet. When the foot is weighted, the ski must also be weighted. A weighted ski cannot be lifted off the ground.

Weight Transfer Shifting weight from one place to another. In skiing, weight is transferred in two ways. It can be shifted from one foot to the other or it can be shifted from one part of the foot to another part (*see* Leverage).

Wind Chill Lowering of the effective atmospheric temperature by the wind.

Index

About the Author

R. J. SANDERS, a Denver surgeon, has been a member of the Colorado Doctors' Ski Patrol for many years. A graduate of the University of Michigan, Dr. Sanders has been on the teaching faculty of the University of Colorado Medical School since 1960. In this book he has combined his background in anatomy and teaching with his years of experience skiing in the mountains of Colorado.

About the Contributors

Several specialists contributed their expertise to the section on health and safety:

Albert Guggenheim, M.D., Clinical Assistant Professor of Medicine, University of Colorado Medical Center and General Rose Medical Center, Denver, Colorado.

Harold Leight, M.D., Associate Clinical Professor of Ophthalmology, University of Colorado Medical Center and General Rose Medical Center, Denver, Colorado.

Barry Lindenbaum, M.D., Clinical Instructor, Department of Orthopedics, University of Colorado Medical Center and General Rose Medical Center, Denver, Colorado.

M. Martinelli, Jr., Project Leader, Mountain Snow and Avalanche Research Project, Rocky Mountain Forest and Range Experiment Station, Fort Collins, Colorado.

Hal O'Leary, P.S.I.A., Director of the Handicap Programs, Winter Park Recreational Association, Winter Park, Colorado.

Mischa Plam, Director of the Mountain Research Center, Institute of Arctic and Alpine Research, University of Colorado, Boulder, Colorado.

Knox Williams, Mountain Snow and Avalanche Research Project, Rocky Mountain Forest and Range Experiment Station, Fort Collins, Colorado.

Phillip S. Wolf, M.D., Associate Clinical Professor of Medicine, University of Colorado Medical Center and General Rose Medical Center, Denver, Colorado.